# THE POET DREAMING
## IN THE ARTIST'S HOUSE

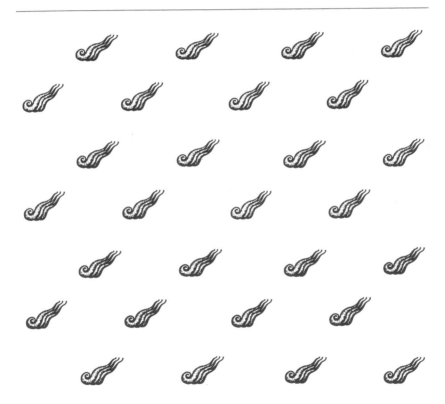

# THE POET DREAMING
## IN THE ARTIST'S HOUSE

Contemporary Poems About The Visual Arts

Edited by Emilie Buchwald and Ruth Roston
Designed and Illustrated by R.W. Scholes

Annotated Bibliography by Phyllis Janik

MILKWEED EDITIONS
1984

Library of Congress Catalog Card Number: 83-73502

ISBN 0-915943-00-X hardcover
ISBN 0-015943-01-8 paper

*This project is supported by a grant from the
Metropolitan Regional Arts Council (with
funds appropriated by the Minnesota State
Legislature), with special assistance from the
McKnight Foundation, and with the aid of
grant support from the Jerome Foundation.*

*First printing: 1984*

*Published by Milkweed Editions*
P.O. Box 24303
Minneapolis, Minnesota 55424
Manufactured in the United States of America

For Poets and Artists

*The world about us would be desolate except for the world within us. There is the same exchange between these two worlds that there is between one art and another, migratory passings to and fro, quickenings, Promethean liberations and discoveries.*

Wallace Stevens

# ACKNOWLEDGEMENTS

We gratefully acknowledge permission to reprint materials from the following sources by these poets:

Judith Berke, "The Red Room," *The Georgia Review*, Vol. XXXVIII, No. 1 (Spring 1984), © by the author. Reprinted by permission of *The Georgia Review*.

Ralph Burns, "Only One," first appeared in *Field*, No. 27 (Fall 1982), and later in *Us* by Ralph Burns (Cleveland State University Poetry Center, 1983), © by the author. Reprinted by permission of the author.

Olga Cabral, "At the Jewish Museum," *The Croton Review*, 1978, © by the author. Reprinted by permission of the author.

Olga Cabral, "Mother and Sister of the Artist." From *In the Empire of Ice* (West End Press, 1980). © by the author. Reprinted by permission of the author.

Olga Cabral, "Picasso's Women." From *Occupied Country* (New Rivers Press, 1976), © by the author. Reprinted by permission of the author.

Criss E. Cannady, "In the Sitting Room of the Opera." From *Lakes and Legacies* (Blue Moon Press, 1978), © Blue Moon Press. Reprinted by permission of the author.

Criss E. Cannady, "Sunlight in a Cafeteria," first appeared in *The Black Warrior Review*. Reprinted in *Anthology of Magazine Verse and Yearbook of American Poetry* (Monitor Book Company, 1980), © by the author. Reprinted by permission of the author.

Diana Chang, "Trying To Change." *Milkweed Chronicle* Vol. 4, No. 3. (Fall 1983), © by the author. Reprinted by permission of the author.

Joan Colby, "Equestrienne" and "The Magician." From *Chagall Poems* (The Seven Deadly Sins Press, Nacogdoches, Texas, 1980), © by the author. Reprinted by permission of the author.

Philip Dacey, "Edward Weston in Mexico City." From *How I Escaped from the Labyrinth And Other Poems* (Carnegie-Mellon University Press, 1977), © by Philip Dacey. Reprinted by permission of the author.

Frank Graziano, "The Potato Eaters," first published in *The Beloit Poetry Journal*, © by the author. Reprinted by permission of the author.

Patricia Hampl, "An Artist Draws A Peach." From *Woman Before An Aquarium* (University of Pittsburgh Press, 1978), © by Patricia Hampl. Reprinted by permission of the author.

Edward Hirsch, "Matisse." From *The Sleepwalkers* (Alfred A. Knopf, Inc., 1976) © by the author. Reprinted by permission of Random House, Inc., Alfred A. Knopf, Inc. and Pantheon Books.

Phyllis Janik, "Sleeping Peasants," first appeared in *Another Chicago Magazine*, © by the author. Reprinted by permission of the author.

Norbert A. Krapf, "Rural Lines After Breughel," *Poetry*, September 1973, © by The Modern Poetry Association. Reprinted by permission of The Modern Poetry Association.

# CONTENTS

## 2 / SCENES

## 3 / STILL LIVES

## 4 / THE THING ITSELF

# PREFACE

Seeing the world is our principal means of entering into it. The eye takes in line and shape, caresses contour and is stimulated by the play of light and color.

A work of art is seen at once, whole and entire. Although poets have the possibility of suspending a reader in time, they have envied artists this direct and immediate access to sensation and emotion, while they must communicate indirectly through the symbols of written language — hieroglyphs which exclude those who cannot interpret them. "The author is obliged to address himself to the mind before he can address the heart," Paul Gauguin wrote in 1888. Poets, however, have been fascinated by the challenge of making word pictures of works of art for the minds and hearts of readers.

A sketch of the relationship between poetry and the visual arts from classical antiquity to the present, such as Phyllis Janik presents in her annotated bibliography at the conclusion of this book, demonstrates a long and vigorous tradition of this literary pictorialism. Toward the end of the nineteenth century, when both artists and poets had sophisticated their technical abilities to create mirror images of the physical world, artists like Gauguin and the poet Stéphane Mallarmé no longer considered that ability as a worthy aim of art or of poetry. Instead, they believed that only the imagination and the expression of the individual were the proper province of art.

Charles Baudelaire's belief that "the whole of the visible universe is only a storehouse of images and signs . . . that the imagination must digest and transform" was shared by poets such as Paul Verlaine, J.-L. Huysmans and Stéphane Mallarmé, and artists like Gauguin, Odilon Redon, Maurice Denis and Edvard Munch.

In 1914, Franz Marc writes that "the contemplation of the world has become the penetration of the world." Wassily Kandinsky, his friend, and associate in *Der Blaue Reiter* almanac, reiterates the idea that the subject matter and focus of art is "in the mystic content. Everything has a secret soul, which is silent more often than it speaks."

To give voice to the secret soul of things, "to the ghostly aspect of things that only rare individuals see," as Marc Chagall puts it, is the artist's quest. The artist's journey must take him to the innermost sources of creation, Paul Klee believed, "as far as may be toward that secret ground where primal law feeds growth" to "render the secretly perceived . . . visible." These ideas are restated by Howard Nemerov in his poem "The Painter Dreaming in the Scholar's House," from which we take our book's title. A meditation of singular nobility and beauty, written in memory of the painters Paul Klee and Paul Terrace Feeley, this poem might stand as a credo for the ideas of many twentieth century artists who "sing the secret history of the mind." The first verse stanza echoes Klee's words: "The painter's eye follows relation out./ His work is not to paint the visible./ He says, it is to render visible." The vision of wholeness in the artist's mind is the dream, the "emblem to us in this life of thought."

The poets in this anthology write about both historical and contemporary art with the resources and prejudices of the late twentieth century. "Nobody paints as he likes," writes the French artist Jean Bezaine. "All a painter can do is to will with all his might the painting his age is capable of," a statement as true for poets as for painters.

Modern physics has shown that the role played by an observer becomes *part* of the experiment. As one physicist puts it, "the vital act is the act of participation. 'Participator' is the incontrovertible new concept given by quantum mechanics." Studies of the psyche have come to much the same conclusions; we interact with what we encounter. We make a difference in what we see.

These poets are participators rather than examiners or dissociated observers. They choose to walk into the artist's house of vision and visions, seeking language fresh enough and transparent enough to communicate their responses. They use the artist's techniques of collage, of commenting upon a found object, of utilizing accident in composition. Picasso's comment that "the artist is a receptacle for emotions that come from all over the place; from the sky, from the earth, from a scrap of paper, from a passing shape, from a spider's web" is equally relevant for the contemporary poet who projects his spirit into the mysterious and "secret soul" of which Klee writes.

When we read and discussed these poems, they seemed to fall readily into four groupings. "Portraits of the Artist" are reflections on individual artists, and on the character of the artist's achievement. "Scenes" are word pictures of specific settings within paintings. "Still Lives" distill impressions of the subjects and objects depicted in works of art. The fourth section, "The Thing Itself," contains poems which concern the nature of art — its function in the individual's daily life, its relation to external nature, and its necessity as an outpouring of the human spirit.

These poems affirm for us the fact that the impulse to make art and to write poems rises out of the same desire to sing "the secret history of the mind," to extend the boundaries of the imagination and to give us what our lives would be barren without. We invite you to walk through the gallery they represent and to experience their depths, their humor and color, as participants in these visions, not unmoved.

*Emilie Buchwald / Ruth Roston*
*April 1984*

# PORTRAITS OF THE ARTIST

## PICASSO'S WOMEN

*(Picasso is said to have strongly urged his friend, the poet Louis Aragon, to get rid of his wife, Elsa Triolet, because she — Elsa — was growing older . . . )*

In Cagliostro's mirror the magician keeps all his women:

the green woman with plants for fingers
the woman of snowstorms; calm flakes fall from her eyelids
the woman who leans on her arm; it becomes bread on the table
the woman whose face is a ripe pod just burst open
the woman with the face of several strangers under one hat
the woman all circular arms; the kiss of her face bends over
the woman whose face grows roots like a vegetable
the woman whose head floats off as her shoulders leave the room

women made of fruit women made of machine parts
women's eyes like spiders minerals or medallions
women's eyes with small wheels whirring behind them
women like walking hieroglyphs of women
women like walking fetishes of rag or of coconut bark
women of fishbone women of cactus
a woman like a watermelon a woman of green rind:
open her face and her rows of black seeds are laughing

The magician has shuffled their features like decks of cards
he wants his women cardboard he wants them Cretan vases
he tosses them noses they catch each other's chins
but no matter how he deals the One-Eyed Woman always turns up
she of the double profile who watches both ways:
the archetypal ancestress changing but changeless

knowing the ripe peach is a guttering candle
knowing the pitcher is pouring its own clay
knowing the flowers are lamps blowing themselves out
the women watch from Cagliostro's mirror
as the magician slowly turns into a piece of sundried driftwood
under the grave eyes of women forbidden to age

## TO MARK ROTHKO OF UNTITLED (BLUE, GREEN), 1969. AMERICAN 1903-70. *Oil on paper mounted on linen*

Never this scratched world, its human
brows like dry point, your harmonies
are liquid glycerin, soothing,
the lingering bath.  Who knew
better than you, Mark Rothko:
color has not root nor core.
Into each other at the first
kiss fusing, a metamorphosis!
Blue paint laps about our toes,
our skin is going deep deep green —
the wild smell, the spruce,
the evergreen pricking its cool needles.

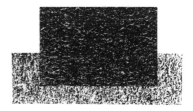

## *TO MORRIS LOUIS OF THE* BLUE VEIL *1958-9.* AMERICAN *1912-62. Acrylic resin paint on canvas*

No longer tension, no dimension, only the words without letters
floating in their washes, hiding Salomé,
the figure behind our musings
trapped in her camouflaging dance.
The limit makes the shape
and we have none,
no bodies for the indistinct yearnings
ebbing into mist, desire and mist.
Imagine the sea without a surface,
the sky without a sun,
and no earth at all,
only the light
blending into pigments
and arching back again.

## TO HELEN FRANKENTHALER OF CIRCE, 1974.
## AMERICAN 1928-
*Acrylic resin paint on canvas*

The fire, the dusky waterlily edge on the horizon
erect, examining the realm of Circe
a sea-animal flicks to and fro
now here, now out of reach
"Come to me," yearns Circe
round red mouth bleeding song
like night jasmine
"I reveal you to yourself
I tell you what to know beyond
the curtain of flame, the mottled flower
beyond the painter's brush
which cries Form! Form!
I dissolve you in my breath
I wind you to my weather."

## LITTLE ROACH POEM
### for Bliem Kern

either he is an excellent critic
or is blue-sensitive
or perhaps he is the six-legged spirit
of the painter himself.

I mean Bliem, of course.

for he goes straight down along
the sun-colored wall of my foyer,
climbs up on to that watercolor,
circles it tentatively,
and then climbs the little palm tree there
leaning out to sea.

he waves his delicate antennas like radar
at passing ships,
a tiny roach castaway
in a blaze of yellow.

so I think of Bliem this morning
sitting framed in his high window
peering out over the Hudson
at the passing tugs and barges
and painting and painting and painting himself

into a blaze of sunlight
over a blue sea.

## DÜRER'S PIECE OF TURF

He rose like a sleepwalker just
before the sun, walked beyond
the city walls with a spade,
dug up a clump of turf dripping

with dew.  In the pale light
he carried the turf through
the arched gateway, tiptoed up
the back stairs, set it before

him at eye level.  He looked.
Sunlight trickled through
the window facing him.  He listened.
The city was quiet as an empty church.

He looked again.  He saw dandelions
with florets closed like fists.
Moisture slid along the veins of great
plaintain.  He blinked, noticed

a shoot of yarrow.  He looked once
more, picked up a brush, stroked
in what he'd seen.  He looked back,
filled in meadow grass, cock's foot,

heath rush.  He laid down long shafts
with quick strokes, dabbed on seeds
and closed blossoms, added white roots
curling like worms out of dank earth.

He paused, lowered his brush, examined
his watercolor, and felt a flash
of summer.  Sunlight splashed onto his
cheeks and hair.  He rubbed his eyes.

He looked up, squinted into the sun.
He heard cries on the street below,
the clomping of hoofs, the rattling of pans,
and the bells of St. Sebald's Church.

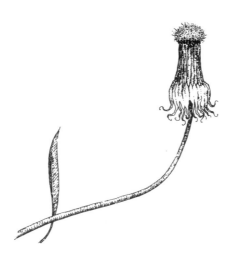

## WOMAN PAINTER OF MITHILA

A small girl, I knelt
over scraps of paper,
and drew the gods
as my mother taught me:
Blue Krishna, holding a flute,
and the lovers, Rama and Sita.
My ink was soot, my brush
threads plucked from my sari.

When a man was chosen for me
I lifted my eyes and saw
the god in him.  Curls
of night-black hair on his nape.
Thin fingers that could coax
a lizard from its stone.
I ground bright earths for paint,
powdered sandalwood and pollen,
mixed them with goat's milk.
I gave him a comb
wrapped in a picture of serpents and flowers.

Now the moon
is in her last phase
and I have started to paint the wall of our hut
with the ancient wedding spell:
on a field the color of blood,
a lotus unfolds its petals, pierced
by a slender shaft:  the god and goddess.

It does not matter
that the wall will be washed,
the colors fade.  For four nights
while the ashes of our marriage fire
grow pale
my love and I will sleep
in these red fields of god,
chaste and burning
as stars.  Then we will dance
to the music
of his flute.

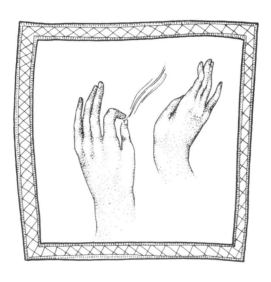

## SHAMAN: *for Malcolm*

He comes in the spring,
spilling his wares
from embroidered bags
and leather pouches:
bracelets of ash wood,
elm chip puzzles, a face
peering out from a hood of bark.
On his fingers are rings
of twisted bloodroot.

Wood finds its way
to his hands, drawn
by the shape-shifter's art
and desire for metamorphosis.
In his pockets lie remnants
of a forest that stretched
to where the ice begins, trees
that were saplings when
the great hunt ended.

He tells of a grim winter,
bobcat tracks in the snow,
and Lucifer the raven
dead of pneumonia. He wears
no animal mask
or cloak of bluejay feathers,
yet for days after he leaves
I find scraps of his art
between pages of books and under
the sofa cushions: mouse bones
carved with glyphs, willow whistles,
and in the potted fern,
greenish, pulsing, a clutch
of snake eggs.

## " . . . THAT FIRST GULP OF AIR WE ALL TOOK WHEN FIRST BORN."
*for Kathleen Zuckerman*

the artist has slipped her spiral shell
and through the water
colors spreading
from her brush
swims down into herself

fluid as fins of angelfish
she flashes    newborn
in that wet world

waves of her hair
shout in the silence
as she dives to the dark
maze of shark's teeth
honed on blood

then rises into filtered light
beneath the surface    full
of herself
and sinuous as an eel
flowing with the tide dance
of kelp

and in that warm drift
of aquamarine    that pulse
of lavender fronds
she finds a home    where
for the first time
she can breathe

## THE PERFECTIONIST

He puts footnotes on the paintings

Hung
he denounces them for refusing
to tell their true story

Will his friends misinterpret?
His world end?

Hung
the damned things seem to take on
lives of their own

On his painting 'The Russian Dancers'
(black booted Cossacks in tall fur hats
crouching in deep knee bend
buttocks sitting on air),
he footnotes:
> 'Their legs erupt
> in split second catapults.'

Rumor has it
he himself hid in the Modern
after hours
& kicked a hole through his
*Late At Night Jam Sessioning Musicians*
for giving out with the wrong combination
of notes

## THE ARTIST

He liked best watching TV
Next was shading all the maps
his father threw at him. — *Maybe*
*you'll learn something despite the tube,*
*you can color them in*
The felt-tipped pens from the studio:
wet black   the deep blues
orange   yellow   kelly green

At first he followed the lines:   France
was purple, Australia blue, all of Russia
a deep brown, not red.   But soon the colors spilled
over the lines and over each other:   a mess
His father was a successful artist. — *Successful*
*artists are stronger than their children, otherwise*
*you kids gobble us up*
white green yellow grey red blue black black black

He'd move through the spectrum warm and cool
darker and darker toward the center:
country   state   city   street   home
Nothing in this world   blacker
than his room.   Even his father couldn't find him here
*Color is psychological* his father said
*Pink is the color of laughter*
black white green yellow grey red red

When he turned off the TV
he would fall into that little white dot
and pop through the screen
to the nowhere where nobody lived.
Intensity is what he was after.

## THE POTATO EATERS

*. . . those people, eating their potatoes in the lamplight, have dug the earth with those very hands they put in the dish . . .*

van Gogh

Prologue

Contrary to popular belief, the potato (also called the common potato, white potato, and Irish potato), is unrelated to the sweet-potato and yam, but is distant kin to the tomato, red pepper, tobacco plant, and eggplant. The potato (derived from the Spanish *patata*, itself stolen from *batata*, the American Indian name for the unrelated yam), although of the top eight food-crops of the world, differs from the others in that the edible portion of the plant is a tuber, that is, the swollen end of an underground stem, anchored to its task of nutrition. The earth, then, is in some sense a straight-jacket, and the potato, like the agitated catatonic patient, is bound indefinitely to its quarters. Already the pity begins.

The potato has a corky skin pierced by lenticles through which occurs gaseous exchange. The stems, usually angular in section, vary in posture, thickness, color (ranging from green to deep purple), pubescence, and other characteristics. The corolla of the flower is wheel shaped, five-lobed, 2-3 centimeters in diameter, and varies in color from white or pale yellow to deep reddish or bluish purple, often tipped or striped with white. The peasant woman, Gordina de Groot, has breasts the color of a dark soft soap, full-blown lips, a dirty cap, and a heart which, despite its lifeblood, is a melanotic cave filled with candles. The tubers bear spirally arranged "eyes" in the axils of aborted leaves, of which scars in the flesh remain.

Potatoes, lovers of armor, can be thought of as underground reservoirs of light, or water mixed with light, the way sometimes a full moon falls into a pond, and the two blues mingle their hues. But the potato, above all is a laboratory, a conservatory dedicated to the study of silence, to the conversion of sound into a starchy pulp; it is a chamber fermenting bass cellos and drums, rehearsing for opening night.

And the earth, by nature, prefers this silence, the same drab hush of *solanum tuberosum*, the same mime, the same earth-pockets of pity. And it is not for the tongue caked with *au gratin* that the potato persists with its profound silence, its crippled, but not full immobile glow, like that of a candle in blubber. It is for the root-haired hand shoved down in the earth,

and the ear in sand, and the tongue that sucks that heart from each stone-
crumb, each potato-steamed molecule floating from the pot, each moment
in the potato-lit cottage.


1.
Sundays
the palms came down
from the cross.

No, not really,
but today a bougainvillaea
dangled its bracts, while in the sun
a dead wren
and the earth attached,
a claw,
bloodstiff, held an unseen
perch, blossomed
in the shape
of grapes.  Sometimes
resting
in the dusk-red fields
I would
raise the enduring gulch
of my hand, and imagine
a glove-white
flesh
on the palm, a nail-hole gnawed
the way a moth
chews worsted, "Life

is no palindrome,"
the painter said
the Lord
said, but with a backhanded stroke
I rubbed the breast
of the wren, and closed the misguided
claw
with my hand, as though wrapping a mesquite twig
in leather.

2.
I might have dried
the breast
in the sun, or boiled the claw for bouillon
or broth, or cupped
the corpse
in these root-fond hands, hurled it
to the air
for flight.  But with a stone
I dug
beneath the stump on an oak, and buried
the wren
in the loam-lined earth, and walked, while
the dead moon
wobbled alone, with the Christ-hole bored
in my hand.  And evenings
I would hold the wound
to my eye, like a lens, as though a nail
really pierced
my fusiform palm, and a world-
heart
pulsed beyond the unbroken
hand:  a reed
fence girdling a lilac plowland, and meat,
and a fog descending
on the fleece of lamb . . . my
breasts
might weave against the sky
in blossom
but in the cottage on earth,
potatoes.

3.
Unsuited
for the dream-life beyond
the hand, the rosebush, the beehives
dripping from their seams
with honey, unsuited
I buried

the hole in my palm, and sealed the lid
on my fuscous eye, and arched
my fingers
in the shape of stone,
and dug into the side
of morning.  I wanted to praise
the hair
on my arms, the languid sun
manuring
the horizon, the fenestral yoke
of this virgin's
egg, root-rotted for lack of fondling.
I wanted
to suck the earth with my face, and cool
my lips with a bluish
mud, and displace
the earth's thinning glaze
of sperm, and retrieve and cradle
a tuber.  And hold it
in praise
like an angel's flesh, and pull it
inside the nest
of the heart, and wrap my yoke
around its crust
of light, and bleed on the nightshade
in mourning.

4.
And evenings gathered
around the rot-
wood table
we would rootle our toad-
colored hands in the dish, like otters
into a pond, or clumps of earth uprooted
also, returning to define
their crop.  And with respect
for the uniform shape
of water

we would hold each potato
like the breast
of a dove, and chew, forever, each mouthful
of pulp, and look only at the air,
forever. I must have closed
my eyes to the dusk, and laid my unambergrised heart
to the earth, and wrapped, in love,
the rector
of the church, and arched each nipple
toward his tongue. And evenings gathered
around the rot-
wood table I would stare past the steaming
disciples
of the moon, and past the unending
gray
in the oil-lamp's light
which, to the untrained eye,
seems white.

5.
Dear Theo,

The hands, especially, have greatly changed. I have found them in lamplight. Brown and green. I shall lend my brush to the air of this earth. And
the potatoes. And two cottages, half-moldered beneath the same thatched
roof, were an odd couple, worn with age, who have grown like praying
hands into one being, and are seen leaning into each other.

Good-bye, with a handshake,

Vincent

## AN ARTIST DRAWS A PEACH

She wanted to depict man and woman
so she started with a snake.
It was green and flat as a ribbon.
It wasn't right, there was no curve
for a belly, no green under the green.
Even the huge apple had no far side to its red moon.

She was alone, she was willing to wait.
Then she saw the peach.
It held out its peach color.
She drew it, drew it out
of her body, it was the color
of the secret places of her body.
Was anyone else peach-colored
and bulging with another surface?

She incised the peach with a hairline stroke,
its pink split like a bivalve in water,
like her own buttocks; she could
breathe deeply again, the pink was released.
It folded its peach smoothly,
it bent toward its other side,
the flesh lit a candle under its skin.

Now she had teeth,
her tongue touched her own body.
I was so afraid, she said,
but the peach, it was the first
thing I really drew.  I understood
its color.  As for shape,
the shape was in the color.
My own body spoke
from its long shyness.

## MATISSE

To begin with a light as vivid and warm
As the strong brown hands of my mother
Braiding my grandmother's hair
For a Saturday night dance in the country.
All over the house there are preparations:
In the basement my grandfather is soaping
His gray beard in a thick mist rising
From the water in a steamy iron tub;
Upstairs my sister is trying on her pink shoes
And red slip, and her red shoes and
Pink slip, and her orange dress. Outside
I am watching my peasant friend Talosha
Trying to teach my eldest brother Claude
A real Polish polka. Father says it is
As hopeless as trying to teach a French pear
Sapling to grow Moroccan apples. Everyone laughs.
Everyone. I'd like to begin with a light
As warm and vivid as that laughter.

And I'd like to end with the red interior
Of an enormous country house blazing with lights
For the dance. My grandfather is wearing
A string tie someone sent him from America,
My grandmother is drinking real peach brandy
In a coffee cup. My mother is dressed
In a dress the color of crushed strawberries
And my sister has decided on a navy skirt
With a red sash and a bright red scarf tied
Around her neck. Even my brother can't take
His eyes off her. And me? Well, I'm drunk.
I am whirling around and around the dance floor
With Talosha until the bright peasant blouses
Become a steady blur circling on the walls,
A dizzy whirling of lights and stars. And then

My father carries me upstairs and puts me
In an enormous double bed with satin sheets,
And then nothing else but sleep.  And this:

All night I hear the music in my head;
All my life I dream of dancers whirling
Through the trees like colorful wild beasts.

## THE EDWARD HOPPER RETROSPECTIVE

The man's dead
so I suppose that any looking
at the paintings
*must* be backwards
though I read someplace that
even when alive, he often held
the paintings back
unsigned, few dates
stuck in back rooms
didn't say much about it
never spoke much at all
married late, precipitating
his sensual period
painted the wife a few times
and let her do the talking
when the guests dropped by.

Today in Pasadena, two earnest gents
with full gray heads
one electric as Einstein's
both in shirts and slacks pressed
sharp and clean as the neighborhood Chinese
could squeeze it
scuttle and murmur through this gallery.
Old Left, I figure
readers of Fearing
totalling between them maybe
six or eight votes for Norman Thomas.
"He said it right in this one,"
one gent says
and the other nods
and they both stand there
looking and nodding
at a barren gas station
on the wall in Pasadena —

and I'm thinking
what do these gray gents see
that famous Hopper loneliness
some moody Americana?
do they picture Tom Joad stopping for a fill-up?
Dillinger knocking over the joint for pocket money?
what did Hopper trigger right in that one
something from a film or book?
or some gas station they remember
thirty, forty years ago.

That solitary painter, these eminent gents
an art museum in Pasadena.
I try to find
the proper retrospective.

## THE PHOTOGRAPHER

After rain he ventures out
across the field,
tripod and camera
floating above his head
like a periscope.
The tall weeds and grasses
slant the way the rain fell,
slowing his stride.

He is going west
with the low sun
to a place meant for light
diffused by distant rain
and a scattering of thin clouds,
light that even now
is flowing down
as if on slow currents of air
to flood the field warm and yellow,
light that draws from him
like a poultice
some essence of himself.

## THE ONE WHO GREW TO BE A WOLF

The fall that she turned fifty
there were no blueberries. The
zucchini failed. The lettuce
overwhelmed us all with transience.

For months she dreamed of nodding yellow
daisies. One night something stirred dark
beneath the flowers; she saw; she
grew thin; her paintings bloomed.

And then she ran into the forest
near her home and was gone all
night and all the next day and just
when the search-party was ready

she trotted out. A breathless
shadow strode with her. She changed
her name to Movement-Under-Flowers
and now she paints huge landscapes

stabbed with the shadow light of wolves.

## EDWARD WESTON IN MEXICO CITY

Clouds, torsos, shells, peppers, trees, rocks, smokestacks.
Let neither light nor shadow impose on these things
To give them a spurious brilliance or romance,
Let the mystery be the thing itself revealed
There for us to see better than we knew we could.
The pepper. The simple green pepper. Not so simple.
There are no two alike. Sonya brings me new peppers
Every day and each one leads me to the absolute
In its own way. My friends tell me the peppers
I've done cause physical pain and make
Beads of sweat pop out on the forehead. Orozco,
As soon as he saw them, said they were erotic.
I know nothing of that. I only know
Or seek to know the inner reality
Of each particular fruit, the secret
It tries but fails to hide because
In truth it would be known and taken;
The secret is of itself and beyond itself.
This pepper here:  follow its form
And you enter an abstract world,
Yet always what you are making love to
Is pepper, pepper, pepper. It can both be
And not be itself.
                    The naked female body
When looked at in the right, that is the askew, way
Can also disappear while remaining fully
Present. Yesterday Tina was lying naked on the azotea
Taking a sun-bath. I was photographing clouds.
Then I noticed her and came down to earth
To shoot three dozen negatives in twenty minutes.
It was Tina I took, yet, in this picture,
Her right hip rises to become a slope
On the other side of Nature, and the ribs
The ribs are hesitancies, a fineness that will go

Only so far amidst the mass then wait
To be discovered by the quiet ones.
Tina, hello and goodbye, and hello.

Just don't ask me to make a formula of this.
With a formula I'd catch only the appearance
Of a secret. But I must disappoint my friends
By always starting over again, day after day,
So that they say, "That's not a Weston, take it out!"
When the sun rises, I become ignorant again,
Unburdened of yesterday's victories. Today
It has been shells. Two shells, one a
Chambered Nautilus. I balanced them together,
One inside the other. White background, black background.
I even tried my rubber raincoat for a ground.
The shells would slip near to breaking.
I am near to breaking, too. That is my formula.
No, I break. I lose myself in the shells.
My friends are right, it's not a Weston, I'm gone,
Thank God. Gone into the luminous coils.
A coil's urge is to be become a circle;
I'm what the coil needs to close the gap.
Pepper, torso, shell: they're circle, circle, circle.

And now for sleep. I'm going to look at the dark.
When I wake up, I won't know what I've seen
But I'll have seen it nevertheless. Tomorrow
I'll look at what's under the sun; if I see right,
I'll be remembering what I see tonight.

# SCENES

## MOUNTAINS AND OTHER OUTDOOR THINGS
### To Lois Dinnerstein, wife of the painter

You like them in pigment
earthworm browns silvered and blunt
out of a tube
not erupted pouring firing forth
then frozen to solid
with rocks that are bleached
to no color.
And the sky, you like it near white
with far away clouds
piled up in mounds on a flat
stroke of sea
while a daub of a ship
goes on its way
which is not a real way
but a course that turns
on its heel
with every new wall.
And the trees you prefer lion dun dim
behind a lavender snood
and plum fan
not intrusively dappled or gnarled crying
"Name me!  My history is traced
in my leaf."
Curled on your couch like a bee
in a yellow light pool
you scan full color pictures
which drift down from your skirts
to the wind's vast museum
finding nature enchanting.
Indifferent to weather
(your face flashes white as new canvas
stacked loose between chairs),
you have thrown in your lot
with the painters,

a menacing bunch who steal
the sun's gold,
black from the elbowing shags,
the Morfo's astonishing blue
(that cloaked bishop of flame)
to condense the background of man
to a frame.  And oh how the fooled
eye loves to rejoice
at the artifice
when the fly is emerald and crisp
and the sunbeam on the checkered floor
asks your hand to slice through it with shade.
But on canvas defiant birds stir,
cracking paint

## KANDINSKY: "IMPROVISATION NO. 27"

A bull.
A fence.
A monk.
An angel in despair.

A bull's nostrils singed with blood.
A fence that separates a torso
from the green of its grave.
An angel in despair.

Blood cascading through a bull's hot brain.
A fence with honed pickets.
Torso of a monk.
An angel in despair.

A bull wrinkled with death.
A monk meditating on death.
A fence capable of death.
An angel impossible in death.

A bull with hot wings stampeding in its pasture.
A monk blinded by his search for wings.
A fence of stakes crossed like wings.
A wingless angel despairs.

Bull.
Fence.
Monk.
Angel: eternally in despair.

## THE SLEEPING GYPSY — *a painting by Rousseau*

Downwind the lion catches scent,
the draw of water, man-smell, the sand
as cool as sleep, the moon-reflecting
moon.  His eyes as white as fear,

at the river drinks beside the sleeping man
who holds a staff to hound off death.
In dreams the gypsy's fingers make a music
on the strings where music sleeps.

To wake would bring these hungers face to face
but the clutch of sleep and thirst play on,
and though death kiss his shoulders
the gypsy cages lions in a song.

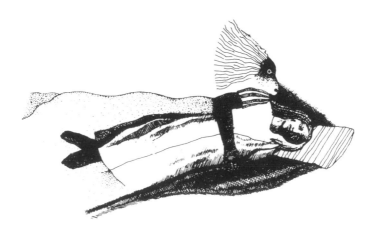

## SLEEPING PEASANTS

A tumble of arms and legs led to this
vigil before deep colorful sleep
— on any ordinary day merely personal,
human, so much of one hump of nothing
but a mess of meat and seasonings
patted into a lumpy form
under a cabbage blanket.

But look at them — the pencil strokes
of his neck, the lines of her red nostrils.
Cross-hatchings of their lights and darks
are brilliant straws, a tangle of pick-up sticks.
His straw hat protects him, blue in shadow
while she gapes open-faced beneath,
baring her left breast and nosing a day-moon,
the moon when the ponies shed.
His toes, her elbows, splayed.  Her blouse,
her green and blue skirt going crazy with creases.

Otherwise it's peaceful, their dream of trudging around,
doing nothing, shining above the clouds
like mounds of gold they've collapsed on.
Caught breathless they're easily carried
over a cloud tundra of wind and snow,
past the swimming iceberg clouds
where every now and then something surfaces
— small fog, a commotion of white bear
that can smell them twenty miles away.
Above their cloud tundra the real moon gapes.
The moon when the ponies shed.

She rests on a trickle of red, her headscarf.

All Pablo did was take a look at their hands, those mouths
and mixed his eggs, colors, water, pencils
and their thick legs. Hers hooked over the hay or bean bags.

It could be they're at rest, finally,
in Lincoln Park, or on his floor in Brighton
or her living room couch, someplace
in or near Chicago — never mind the barn
in the background.  All that matters is
you recognize them.  He did.

Sleeping peasants.
Lovers of the same village.

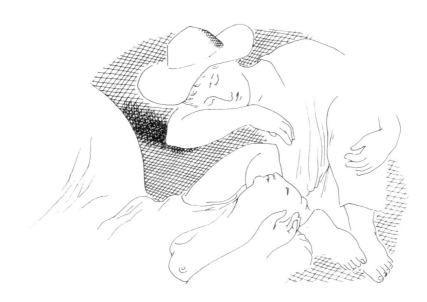

## THE GREAT WAVE OFF KANAGWA
*Woodcut. Hokusai, 19th century.*

You can't escape
the rhythm of this wave, the trough dipping
under the two boats, while
to the left the large ribbed crest
of tsunami rises over them like the inside of a gigantic
black shell.
Motionless, yet it grows
under the eye like a relentless crescendo.
You take in your breath
at the size and you hold it to listen for the sound
of water;
the seductive whisper, the susurration
of the moving wall as it gathers and builds, then breaks
into fine white fingers.
Yet silent, this wave, and the air birdless, empty.
In the sky, only one voice, not water
but mountain; Fujiyama rising from the land.  And the men
in their frail boats
bow their heads and wait.

## HOKUSAI'S WAVE

The two opponents
brace
the wave
gathers itself
slowly climbing the air

and the boat
climbs the vast cliff
of water

steeper and steeper
the endlessly unfolding
fluid and glassy
slopes

but the glittering arch
does not fall
the boat
will not break

there is only one wave
in the universe
and Hokusai is
master of it.

## FOLLOWING VAN GOGH (AVIGNON, 1982)

Sun claims these streets
as it claimed the painter, forever
in love with a land of chalk stone,
cactus and melons.
I could spend years here, with you,
an old woman asleep in doorways
of the last century.

Heat fixes these images,
at noon the shadows
black along the walls,
taste of pressed lemons
we drank all afternoon,
the way the sudden red of geraniums
astounds the eye.

Is it this we look for, this light,
in the painted lines of cypress,
the women stooping over ripe grain?
Another way of seeing;
the painterly touch
of a stranger's hand
in your hair, at night
in the hotel of the world.

## THE RED ROOM

What Matisse could have done
with this miserable afternoon!
First of all he would blur the couple's faces.
Then take out other distractions
like flying dishes, howls, screeches, clocks.
Then he would paint everything red:
the walls, tables, the cat, the couple's hair —
red as an open mouth.
Then he would move the man to a lake
where he would drop stones —
his face scattering and coming together in the water.
The woman would sigh,
an aura around her
like the infinite scrollwork of trees.
A small figure — closed as a Japanese fan.

And yet there would be hope.
The tablecloth alive on the table.
Bushes, clouds, the sky
trembling at the window
as if waiting
for the woman to realize her grace
as she bends there.
For the man to come back —
as sweet in her eyes as the darkening lake.
For the child to wake
from his dreams of blackness and blood and silence.
For the world to come into this red room
without smashing the delicate glasses.
The sun first
carefully through the panes.
Then the man — large and dark in the doorway,
and the cat leaping,
and the red suddenly quivering
in the woman's cheeks.
Like that part of the fire that remains longest.

## TWO WINDOWS BY MAGRITTE

i
We see only his back.
A man not young, not old
stands looking out.

An apple larger than a mountain
floats above his head, green
and perfect loneliness.

ii
No one is at the window now.
Just long loaves of bread
the sky has dreamed.

God knows how many
lonely men the loaves
have eaten.

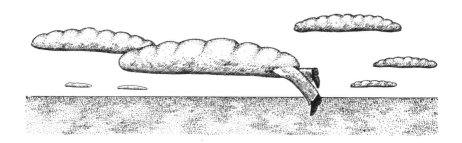

## PASTORAL
*for Kaldis*

Mountain
rises out of paper
purple as in the full
flush of rain
with cap of gold
& brows of curling
knee-high juniper.  Each
touch is explosion of
cypress & thumb-pressed
olives, against which the red,
blue gestures of the houses stand
stiff, hieratic, caught atilt
in a splatter of descending
white-hued steps.
Over it the breath of a broom
swings / swings
& becomes sailcloth, bay
full of kelp, bathing suits,
oven-green laughter;
& the mountain rides
afloat in its dream of
lava, slopes
gathering under it meadows
of tubeless down, cut &
poppy-singed,
where only the breadth
of a cypress sways
& invisible
among almonds
a ploughman whistles.

## ENTERING THE ROOM
*After a photograph by Jack Welpott*

I find the door standing open
like a time exposure,
early morning somewhere in France.
I enter the room as easily as light,
her back to me as she parts
her legs to dry herself,
fresh from the bidet.
In a moment she will look up
and see me in the mirror,
the sudden intake of breath
like the sound of a shutter closing,
and something new will begin
though nothing like what you are thinking.

## WHAT I SAW IN OCTOBER

Three figures rise into a dirty gold field.
Seven angels rise to sing their freedom.
Seven people on a street note
the immanence of arrival but stay below.
The field might be a building.  Rare windows
and a halo or two reflect a sort of light.
If you are going to get caught like this, at least you can stand
on your feet like a column, holding up a field,
perhaps a building, and whatever is holy.

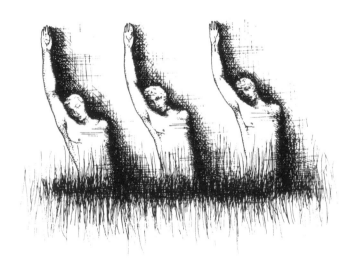

## ANOTHER SUNSET
### For Alvaro Cardona-Hine

One sun has set.  On my wall
another goes on — over a green
and orange earth, the ark
of the faithful, where the goose-
neck shadow of the sun
goes on falling
like a peacock throne
or the sigh of peaches.

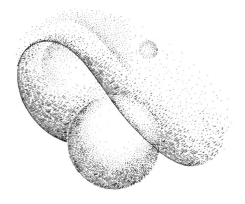

## THE WATER LILY

As slowly, as carefully as a wading bird
The elderly Japanese photographer
Comes down stone steps under leaves through pale-green
    light
To the pond and wavers
At the brink where a single waterlily
White around gold lies open.  Bending, he stares
Long and, bending farther, moves
Along the bankside, pauses again to gaze,
To focus at last, to shift, to hesitate,
To lift his eyes among wrinkles, to lift one shoulder
And one slow corner of his mouth, to take no picture
But slowly to turn away,
To take nothing away but his mind's eye.

## AFTER CHAGALL

Lady, your head is on upside down.
What do you see?

I see a chair, waving its legs.
I see a bird's back.
I see sunflowers standing on their faces
holding up the world.

Here I am, floating through the sky
with my head on wrong
so that my hair tickles my neck
and my chin sticks up,
and the lovers kissing in the garden
look comical, their feet straining
to touch the ground.
It's been a long time since someone
kissed me in the garden.
My mouth's up too high.

I get confused, floating around this way,
and can't always remember if I'm a woman
or a bird.  Birds don't kiss at all.

I see a house falling on a man
sitting near the chimney with a fiddle in his hand.
The man and the house are falling straight at me.
But I'm not worried.
Even though I look at trees
and houses and fiddles and gardens
in a strange, circular way,
I know that up is up and down is down.

It's just that I can't seem to get down
and nothing ever comes up
except a bird, sometimes,
(who doesn't count, because
I'm really a woman).

If I can't reach the garden, I'd like
at least to get to the roof, and sit
and listen to the fiddle.
I'm not asking for kisses,
just a roof under my feet.

## THREE POEMS ON MORRIS GRAVES' PAINTINGS

### 1. *Bird on a Rock*

Poor, thick, white,
three-sided bird
on a rock
(with the big red beak)
you watch me sitting on the floor
like a worshiper
at your melancholy shrine.
All you can do is look.  I mean
you lack any kind of wing or arm
with which to go home.
The three-toed foot of each odd limb
forms a kind of trapezium
about its edge
(though there is no web).
Oh bird, you are a beautiful kite
that does not go up.
You cannot even get down.
Because you've lost your mouth (it's gone)
only your great eyes still moan.
You are filled with the ancient grief,
fixed there lonely as a god or a thief.
Instead of limbs to bring you nearer
Morris Graves has given you
the sudden awful wings of a mirror!

2. *Spirit Bird*

Looking at Morris Graves' Spirit Bird
(1956), suddenly I
understood the structure of angels!
They're made of many colored streams
of the most intense, most pulsing light,
which is itself simply the track
of the seed of God across the void.
Each length of light seems to be a thread
that forms this angelic or spirit
stuff. But it's not. It's finer than that.
What gives the light its substance and shapes
the streams into the spirit thing
(apparent limbs and parts of body)
is the heavy, almost solid and
somehow magnetic *eyes* of angels.
These create the dark into which they glow,
and pull and bend about these sweeps of light.

3. *Moor Swan*

I'm the ugly, early
Moor Swan of Morris Graves.
I'm ungainly, I've got
black splotches on my back.
My neck's too long.
When I am dead and gone
think only of the beauty of my name.
Moor Swan    Moor Swan    Moor Swan.

## RURAL LINES AFTER BREUGHEL

### RETURNING FROM THE HUNT
*for Harry and Hazel Hinchcliffe*

The last specks of sunlight
sparkle in the wisps of snow
balanced on the branches
of the stark, unyielding trees.
Perched way above the action,
crows gaze down coldly upon
a pack of hounds poking their
noses in the crusty snow.
The smell of blood has curdled
in their nostrils; tails curl
with enthusiasm but bottoms
sag. Although already within
the village, they force
a few last hopeful yaps
into the heavy evening air.

Just in front of the hounds
the masters lean their brawny
shoulders into the January
evening. Their boots trudge
homeward in the deep snow.
One man feels the body warmth
of the slain animal slumped
against the small of his back.
From here on it is downhill.
They will coast down to their
cottages and prop their feet
up against a blazing hearth.
After darkness has swooped
down upon the valley like
a vulture, they will consume
rustic food that has simmered

on the fire for hours.  Later
they will go to bed with their
women and know a pleasure which,
like their appetite for food
and the hunt, never diminishes
with fulfillment.  Soon they
will be in the field again.

*HARVESTING WHEAT*
*for Len and Jill Baden*

Mid-August and the sun
has burnt the grain a crackly
brown on the golden stalks.
In slow rocking rhythms
the hatted harvesters curl
their scythes across the base
of the stalks which drop
to the earth with a swish.
The wide path wedged into
the plaited field of wheat
on the near side disappears
as it bends down the ripe
hillside like a snake slithering
into shade. An aproned
woman following the harvesters
bends her body almost double
at the waist until her face
seems to kiss the ground,
then binds with yellow twine
the fallen stalks into sheaves.
Flocked together in scant shade
under a solitary tree, a crew
of sunburnt workers gulps down
their midday meal. They dip
heavy wooden spoons into bowls
of cool porridge, tear off pieces
of bread from thick-crusted
loaves, and suck water from
coiled clay jugs. A full-bellied
man lies snoring on his back
with his head resting up against
the base of the tree. He dreams
of hunting with hounds in the snow.

## A GLOOMY DAY
*for Katherine*

Like a fire about to extinguish,
the March evening flickers with
the last reddish rays of sunlight.
Late winter winds have whipped
the sea in the background to choppy
gray waves.  The mountains squatting
at the side of the harbor shoulder
a load of leaden ivory snow.  Criss-
crossed branches of the still stark
trees are outlined against soggy
dark clouds.  With the smells
of summer still lodged in their
nostrils, the villagers doggedly
go about their daily business.
One man climbs a ladder to mend
the damage storms have done to his
thatched roof.  A neighbor stands
balanced on the rungs of his ladder
brushing white paint onto the weathered
front of his cottage.  In the yard
next door, another man bends down
to the ground to bind a bundle
of twigs for the hearth.  Beside him
his brother stands hunched up against
the trunk of a stubby willow pruning
branches to encourage eventual growth.
They all work with the slow, steady
rhythm of creatures who feel in their
bones a gradual intensification of
daylight and a budding on the branches
high above their heads.  They know
deep in their guts that tomorrow spring
will be one day closer.  That is enough.

## TRYING TO STAY

The next painting, she said to me, should be white

say, a dune picked clean by the sun;
in the upper lefthand corner a scrawl of rushes

or not white at all but that pink and mauve tweed
of a field of potatoes

The sky may be left out or put in
Leeways are sanctuaries of possibility

Try to get the hillock from above
        the way gulls do
You can continue to paint anything at all
but blue and orange and the lavender in shadows
will convey July-ing as though July could be eternal

There are times I know there are too many landscapes;
still she eggs me on.  Far too many

I turn such knowledge like a page.  I don't sit down
        with my life
nearly enough, glade and cove inserted like bookmarks
to keep my place in my reading of this earth

The plants are so still when she closes the windows
but a curator of now wants nothing astir
The sky sits outside the screen door beginning nothing

It's not that I want to fix the light or time or live
forever

We want connection, yes; the traction even of pain,
yes; the tension of chair addressing chair.

When photographs snap up the past, must they make it also dead?
I want those I have known who are gone to be alive again.

The next painting is already gathering dust
The embrace running toward me is already beyond
At love's table tomorrow's wine cuts with acid the sweet grape

But I am, at least, still with myself and talking,
both of us trying to stay well
who move and crave

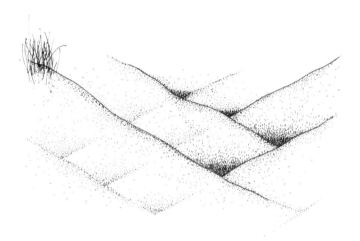

## HOPPER'S "NIGHTHAWKS" (1942)

Imagine a town where no one walks the streets. Where the sidewalks are swept clean as ceilings and the barber pole stands still as a corpse. There is no wind. The windows on the brick buildings are boarded up with doors, and a single light shines in the all-night diner while the rest of the town sits in its shadow.

In an hour it will be daylight. The busboy in the diner counts the empty stools and looks at his reflection in the coffee urns. On the radio the announcer says the allies have won another victory. There have been few casualties. A man with a wide-brimmed hat and the woman sitting next to him are drinking coffee or tea ; on the other side of the counter a stranger watches them as though he had nowhere else to focus his eyes. He wonders if perhaps they are waiting for the morning buses to arrive, if they are expecting some member of their family to bring them important news. Or perhaps they will get on the bus themselves, ask the driver where he is going, and whatever his answer they will tell him it could not be far enough.

When the buses arrive at sunrise they are empty as hospital beds — the hum of the motor is distant as a voice coming from deep within the body. The man and woman have walked off to some dark street, while the stranger remains fixed in his chair. When he picks up the morning paper he is not surprised to read there would be no exchange of prisoners, the war would go on forever, the Cardinals would win the pennant, there would be no change in the weather.

# SEURAT

It is Sunday afternoon on the Grand Canal. We are watching the sailboats trying to sail along without wind. Small rowboats are making their incisions on the water, only to have the wounds seal up again soon after they pass. In the background the smoke from the factories and the smoke from the steamboats merges into tiny clouds above us then disappears. Our mothers and fathers walk arm and arm along the shore clutching tightly their umbrellas and canes. We are sitting on a blanket in the foreground, but even if someone were to have taken a photograph of us only our closest relatives would have recognized us: we seem to be burying our heads between our knees.

I remember thinking you were one of the most delicate women I had ever seen. Your bones seemed small and fragile as a rabbit's. Even so, beads of perspiration begin to form on your wrist and forehead — if we were to live long enough I'm sure we would have been amazed at how many clothes we forced ourselves to wear. At this time I had never seen you without your petticoats, and if I ever gave thought to such a possibility I would chastise myself for not offering you enough respect.

The sun is very hot. Why is it no one complains of the heat in France? There are women doing their needlework, men reading, a man in a bowler hat smoking a pipe. The noise of the children is absorbed by the trees. The air is full of idleness, there is the faint aroma of lilies coming from somewhere. We discuss what we want for ourselves, abstractly; it seems only right on a day like this. I have ambitions to be a painter and you want a small family and a cottage in the country. We make everything sound so simple because we believe everything is still possible. The small tragedies of our parents have not yet made an impression on us. We should be grateful for this, but we are too awkward to think hard about very much. I throw a scaling rock into the water; I have strong arms and before the rock sinks it seems to have nearly reached the other side. When we get up we have a sense of our own importance. We could not know, taking a step back, looking at the total picture, that we would occupy such a small corner of the canvas, and that even we are no more than tiny clusters of dots, carefully placed together without touching.

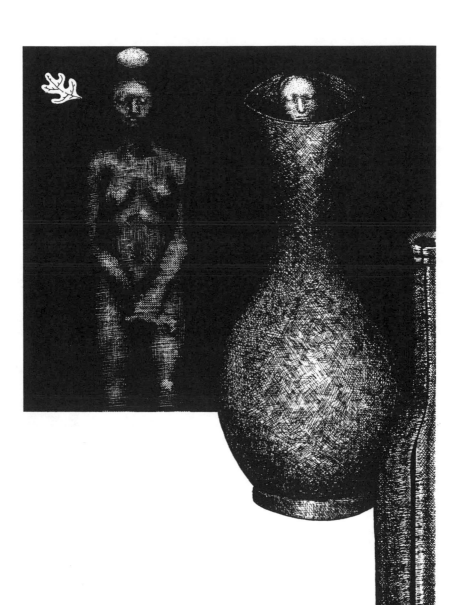

# STILL LIVES

## THE MAGICIAN

Whenever the magician snaps his fingers
a man and a woman lie down together.
The man is lost in love.
The woman winks.

The magician knows another trick.
In this one there are red flowers
to draw the eye from a sleeping city.

Love supplants government,
it knows the powers
of distraction.  You only think
this benevolent bearded man is the magician.

His indigo alter-face
lurks in the wings.

Think of a man's white rabbit.
It disappears
in a woman's black hat.
Everyone gasps.

They want the commonplace
to be extraordinary.
The magician obliges.

The man and woman fall in love.
It lasts.

## *EQUESTRIENNE*

The white horse nuzzles a violin and two pink roses,
the equestrienne holds her red fan.
Her lover exposes her breasts.
The world is watching
breathless.

Does this embarrass you?
You can pretend not to notice,
you can fiddle grey music from a scaffold,
you can dance like an idiot
in a village of goats.

The equestrienne knows that beauty
is the only excuse.  She waits
for your applause.

## FOUR PICTURES BY JUAN, AGE 5

First he made the door, a walk
leading up through trees, each
one like a cloud or cotton on a stick.

Then he drew the roof and chimney,
its skinny smoke curling up and off the page . . .

in back, he wove in hills and mountains,
then the sun, a yellow splash on top,
shining down on flowers and his dog.

When it rained, he crawled inside:
there were no crocks or buckets,
no pots or pans catching water on the floor.

*Send in the clowns,* he'd sing,
*I'm home lying on the rug and it rains!*

Inside by the fire he saw himself
picking ticks off the dog,
then drowning them in the sink.

He never drew the man with a briefcase
knocking at the door,
his parents whispering in the kitchen.

The roof was sound,
nothing dripped, nothing leaked:
posing in the yard,
the family smiled ear to ear.

## THE MAGISTRATE'S ESCAPE
*(after* La Golconde *by Magritte)*

This was a man bivouacked in wool
even on dog days, the magistrate
wearing legal tweeds and the face of a bull.
Bay rum, bay rum, his skin drooled.

This man marched to a trap of dockets
and judicial drabs, the magistrate
envying the birthright of the gulls:
wings to shear the sky's wide pocket.

This was a man of cocktail hours, agog
and swaddled in legal briefs, the magistrate
with the clout of bulls.
He, Nature, God: wheels instead of cogs.

This man invented propellors
above his bifocals, the magistrate
who escaped, freefell like a tarred gull:
a sky scraper among skyscrapers less stellar.

## WOMAN ASLEEP ON A BANANA LEAF
### *from a Chinese painting*

Who wouldn't want such a bed?
In the heat of the afternoon, in a private shade,
she has hidden herself away
like a long, translucent, emerald-spotted snake
her skin a ripple, her spine
curved against the long green spine of this leaf.
Now let the ladies call from their silk pavilion,
and let Lord X compare someone else's skin
to the petals of peonies and other
appropriate seasonal flowers.
She dreams of skin that is cool and green and secret.
When she wakes up she will be completely happy.

## LEDA AND THE SWAN
*on looking at Tintoretto's "Leda and the Swan"*
*in the Uffizi Gallery, Florence.*

Well, of course,
Right by her bed, she did —
kept him in a wicker pen
after he came down in that hot rush
and proved so successful.
Fed him tortellini in cream
sponged him in white wine
took him to Venice for the holidays
to paddle in the canals
and sing along with the boatsmen.
But his was a swan's song, after all
and he drooped over his feed.

And so at five, when the sun comes
honey-slant over the Ponte Vecchio
she'd open the shutters
lie back on the red silks
dressed only in pearls
and the Florentine chiaroscuro
making the room reel with her flesh
as if she fed on ivory,
and fondled his feathers.

But he, like any Greek,
wanting only what he cannot have,
nibbled at her breast,
sighed, and like Odysseus
wished for home.

## WINSLOW HOMER, PRISONERS FROM THE FRONT

For the Union:  a young true-blue
executive, dressed for office,
tallies bodies quick or dead,
computing profits from a profitable risk,
the first of many such, as wars
become immortal while men are not:

and for the South:  graybeards in rags;
hungry, hunchback-clumsy schoolboys
with half a uniform; squirrel guns
starved for bullets, lugged from the boondocks
by slouching backwoods Dixie-whistling poorwhites, and

that one insouciant longhaired brevet-colonel
(cool, erect, indifferently polite
toward conquerors) far from his hounds,
his gelding, his colonnaded house
beyond an avenue of live-oaks
upwind from the barracoons,

who has been out-numbered and out-marshaled,
never outfought, even now become
a nobler part of history:

he of specious might-have-beens
who, like us, has yet to know,
if ever,

the losers from the winners.

## GEO-POLITICS

*after Sebastiano del Piombo's painting "Cardinal Bandinello Saudi, His Secretary And Two Geographers" at the National Gallery of Art*

Bandinello slouches on a chair
facing us in such a way
we read the root of power in his heart

he has stopped listening to the visitors
to taste a particular moment
tucked away in a convent

*only death can slap this longing from my soul* he thinks
and the smile reverberates in Washington
where the painting holds
a subliminal green of the Indies as backdrop
to underlings measuring the world

*to look for grief is the only sorrow* he concludes
and wonders if the Pope
would welcome the bon mot next Saturday at supper

only the careful viewer will notice
by his knee
on those pristine robes
how Sebastiano del Piombo
with the accuracy of a Chinese Zen master answering a student
has painted a fly

## SNOW QUEEN'S PORTRAIT
### for Dahl Delu

I
Snow Queen, crowned
With a single snowflake
Hand of ice around a boy's throat
Glances warily into warm air
Safe from behind glass.
One day, sure of the way to winter,
She'll turn
White robes whipping in the wind
To fly north
With the frozen boy beneath her arm,
Leaving a blank black canvas on the wall.
Frost gathers on the surface of the glass.

II
Over my bed watches the Snow Queen
Diamond hearted crystal crowned
Hexagrammatic over my dreams.
Beyond the walls icicles grow head down
From the eaves to bar the windows.

Over my bed watches the Snow Queen
Silver haired face faceted
Bright as the jewel in the center of her crown.
The lines of the flake angle up over her hair
Branching from the brilliant
Radiating cold.

## AMANDA, PLAYING

Amanda is sending messages again,
dances on air.

her fingers touch the piano,
Bach flies out the window
and scatters the birds like a witch.

Ben's hands are like cats
where he gets at the canvas
painting
Amanda.

it is cool and dark, it is quiet,
it is lavender, is fake roses,
is her mother's closet,
the tired, old-fashioned, the lonely
dresses,
is a door she dare not . . .
is Ben the other side,
is the dream
tall, is powerful
the sweat, is the power of hands
the rough skin
is his hands, in her hands
the flesh breaking    ice    ice
the warm blood the welling up

is the fleet salamander Bach
at the very tip her arched tongue
his name Ben

## STILL LIFE

I am brooding over a nest of red plums and ruby plums,
A straw nest,
I, a bird of green apples,
I get the smallest one, a yellow-red, under my apple bosom.
Oh you helpless little plums, you are my plum ducklings,
I am a green bird-mother apple,
I will love you forever.

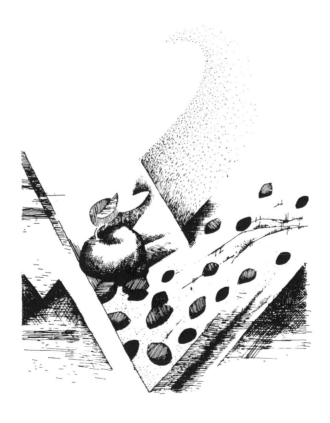

## STILL LIVES

Light ripples lace, glitters from the eaves,
suspends the table in a golden gloom.
Ripeness and warm flesh — a flushed pear's
cheek against a man's blue leather gloves.
Both indifferent to the rose's
lumpish shadow yearning close to theirs.
Behind their backs, the crystal fruit bowl throws
an evil eye, unsheathes its diamond claws.

Longings rise and mingle, real as steam,
a perfume ripe and yellow as the pear's.
The lacquer fan and silver teapot blame
unseasonable weather for these loves,
these hungers trembling in the Flemish air,
this horsefly hovering above the pear.

## IN THE SITTING ROOM OF THE OPERA
### — *after a sketch by Degas*

A young girl holds her left ankle
dreams of Parisian fountains while lifted above
the Prince's head, her arms held out
in waiting.  For this, she forgets
about her foot, her mother dressed
in black, an umbrella's silver tip
drawing circles on the parquet floor.

Her mother's umbrella gets caught
in a notch; once when young
she wanted a man to take her own
slippers off, carry her to a lake
to twirl and skate.  O!  the tiny blades
on her feet!

Now, the shuffle of toe shoes;
pain that has its own sound
only another dancer hears.

*Un, deux, trois* . . .
Still holding her ankle,
the young girl never looks up.
Her mother, who knows about chance,
how it never arrives, is content
to look away from the artist,
from this sketch in pastels;
the browns built up to show
the monotony of waiting.

— *for Bekah*

## SUNLIGHT IN A CAFETERIA
### from a painting by Edward Hopper

Inside this green cafeteria, a woman in blue
stares at her broken nail.  Every afternoon
she fingers an empty glass.  Her saucer burns white.
A diagonal of light leads from a window

to a revolving door where this morning
while her husband read the paper, she ignored
the whistling tea pot, the wilting geranium; looked out
the kitchen window, past the splintering fence

and tall weeds.  Seeing her children, the sun
at their backs, she thought, "Maybe a new hat."
Not blue like the vinyl chairs so neatly
pushed in, but yellow like sunsets seen

in pictures.  If only marriage was like the salt
and pepper shakers placed side by side — a sparkle
of yellow for each angled surface — she would turn away
from the salesman on her left, who is about

to speak, about to offer her a cup of coffee,
a hotel room, large as windows overlooking
old fences, promising as the sunlight, carefully
arranged, cutting her right arm in half.

## MOTHER AND SISTER OF THE ARTIST
### *(Painting by Vuillard. Circa 1893.)*

Voices of vegetables
odor of lamplight
color of camphor

*ma mère, ma soeur*

The mother:  a chest of drawers
in a black dress
an old cupboard somebody has
painted black
years hoarded within her
like coarse but carefully
folded and mended
linen
the key to the cupboard was lost
a long time ago

*Ma mère:*  an uncleared table
her body set with
plates where others
have eaten
her corsets creak like
cellar doors
the black stuff of her dress
is made of whatever
snuffs out candles
with her sturdy foot
she is rocking the cradle
of her old age

The daughter stands beside her
*ma soeur* with the slender
waist and
long white wrists
her hair quivering
fire of copper
pots

Back to the wall
she bends
ready to run but
whalebones corset-covers
rustle of starched underwear
betray her
and she fears the hideous
spotted wallpaper
is eating her up
Those long wrists were surely
meant for something:
domesticity domesticity

Sister do you tire
of the circle of good kind
pumpkin faces?
Do you dream of blue pumpkins?
Do you dream of floating naked
in the net of your hair
on a cold dark river
where fish are saying
your name?

Domesticity domesticity:
there stands the daughter
grown plain as a vegetable
or an old chest of drawers
there sits the mother
slender stark naked
in a net of copper hair

The mother                    her future
the daughter                  her past

Rejoice women:
I have set you in the exact corner
of cruel time

From which there is no escape

## FOLDS OF A WHITE DRESS/SHAFT OF LIGHT
*"The Annunciation"*
*Peter Paul Rubens 1577-1640*

She had been reading, that much we know.
An empty vase beside her book, no one in this story
thought to bring her flowers; she is married,
and her friends are poor.

The angel's cape is a flame, his wild hair a golden fire,
one more angel drops from heaven barefoot, the cobblers sigh.
He is fine, and his gray wings
match his outfit.  She is dressed for a dinner party,
and he flies through the window, drops to his knee,
beseeches her to accept the offer.
She listens, but her heart and hands are stony,
carved and painted into rejection.

She would like to lift her eyes to the baby
angels floating near the ceiling,
she would like to catch the white dove
in her raised hand.
She may be glad the shaft of light turns her white dress
holy, she may not.

Mary, Rubens paints you too grandly
for this myth, you look middle class,
as if you're worrying about where you can place
a sexy man angel at your table, who can talk
small talk with an angel, or make polite inquiries
about celestial weather?

You understand babies though, even floating ones,
and you want the dove to stay near you,
that much is clear, and your blue cloak
cannot protect you from God's demand,
or the strong hand reaching towards
you, about to make you famous
and pregnant.

## THE KISS
### by Edvard Munch

Munch made
man & woman
whole
one
line & loin
hand & hip
breast & rib
entwining
naked
natural
black & white
over & over
again

## THE ANNUNCIATION

In Leonardo's painting, she studies
out of doors, this eminent virgin
in her habitual cloth of red and blue.

Before her on a pedestal table
encrusted with a mollusk shell, lies
an open book from which she raises her eyes

to the boy dressed in swan's wings, wearing
a cap of curls and carrying a wand.
She may have seen him ahead of her

in church, his shoulders and torso
masculine and square, his hair
a tangle of innuendo.

That he comes to her in the garb
of heaven is only an accident
of myth and history, for she needs

nothing announced. The cleft in the palm
of her raised hand anticipates all he means
and she accepts only provisionally,

for he is her inspiration, not a winged
word or an unborn child. This child-man,
with fabulous pinions, will cause her

to abandon the protected corner,
to crush the low, delicate plants
and dream his weight will never rise.

### RILKE SPEAKS OF ANGELS
*From a painting by Lucas van Leyden*
*(1494-1533)*

"Every angel is terrible."
Yet van Leyden's
stands on the crest of a hill,

up which the Flemish road
leads like a lesson,

a league perhaps
from a turreted city,
wherein the Virgin bares
her perfect breast

and whiskery St. Anne
offers wine with arthritic fingers.

His broad nostrils,
auburn hair
have about them earth's

comfort, the familiar
bruising
from which millet rises.

And the mouth "so tired, tired"
forbears to speak

lest the wind from God's
"dark book of origins"
ravage the city, scattering
creation like torn embroidery.

From his shoulders grow
great brows,
marked with a creamy white
meadow plumage.

One hand points
protectingly down.  The other,
heraldic,
soft-padded at base of thumb,

is a cousin of wings.
"Praise this world
to the angel . . . Tell him *things*."

## RENAISSANCE/A TRIPTYCH

### 1 Annunciation

The angel
against a backdrop of gold.
*Ave Maria* . . .
scrolls out of its mouth in darker gold.
Mary, seated, her book about to fall off the table,
knows it's no use to argue.
She looks toward the ground
as the words reach her,
and can't pretend she doesn't understand.

### 2 Annunciation

A second angel
hovering
spreads his arms
and seven rays
shoot toward
the Virgin.
A dove
with a halo
is diving through them.
She gasps
as the sharp points
penetrate her heart
and burn tiny holes
where the swords will later go.

## 3 Leda

Under these beating wings,
her neck caught in his beak.
Half the time she thinks
the earth pushes back
against this bird's weight
and she's caught
between two conspiracies.
What can anyone know
that a god can't
even when he's forgotten
he's a god
and falls in love
with these feathers.
She still can't exactly
implore heaven
*now what about this pain*
*what about this ecstasy.*

## THE POSTCARDS: A TRIPTYCH

The Minoan Snake Goddess is flanked by a Chardin still-life, somber
and tranquil, and by Mohammedan angels
brilliantly clothed and with multicolored wings,
who throng round a fleshcolored horse with a man's face
on whose back rides a white-turbanned being without a face,
merely a white, oval disk, and whose hands too are unformed, or hidden
in blue sleeves.
                    Are the angels bringing attributes
        to this unconscious one?
Is he about to be made human?
                              One bends to the floor of heaven in
                                                            prayer;
one brings a bowl (of water?) another a tray (of food?); two
point the way, one watches from on high, two and two more
indicate measure, that is, they present
limits that confine the way to a single path;
two debate the outcome, the last
prays not bowed down but looking
level towards the pilgrim.
Stars and the winding
ceintures of the angels surround
the gold cloud or flame before which he rides; heaven itself
is a dark blue.
                    Meanwhile the still-life offers, makes possible,
a glass of water, a wine-bottle made of glass so dark it is
almost black yet not opaque, half full of
perhaps water; and besides these, two courgettes
with rough, yellow-green, almost reptilian skins,
        and a shallow basket
of plums, each almost cleft
with ripeness, the bloom upon them, their skin
darker purple or almost crimson where a hand
touched them, placing them here.  Surely
this table, these fruits, these vessels, this water
stand in a cool room, stonefloored, quiet.

And the Goddess?
                    She stands
between the worlds.
                    She is ivory,
her breast bare, her bare arms
braceleted with gold snakes.  Their heads
uprear towards her in homage.
Gold borders the tiers of her skirt, a gold hoop
is locked round her waist.  She is a few inches high.
And she muses, her lips are pursed,
beneath her crown that must once have been studded with gold
she frowns, she gazes
at and beyond her snakes as if
not goddess but priestess, waiting
an augury.
                    Without thought I have placed these images
over my desk.  Under these signs
I am living.

---

## WARRIOR WITH SHIELD
### (Henry Moore, 1953)

1

As if he had crawled from the sea.

Like a son beaten down
by the dark father century
or by the mother of centuries mutilated

he sits.

He will not go back to that sea
though his bronze reminds me
of its weeds crushed inward.

It seems he could yet swivel,
that with the one good arm
and shield clipped onto muscle
he still could sweep an enemy away.
Whoever hacked him elsewhere
should step with care here.

Eyes holes.  Mouth a small
star-burst, as when a meteor
hurts the earth.
Where halves of the face should meet,
where there should be seam —

fissure.

As if with our own hands
we might complete you.
As if you had crawled to us for completion.
As if you were ours to grow.

2.

*No more*
*to wither in me.  No more*
*to be made of me.*

*Nothing*
*for fathering, mothering.  Done.*
*Caresses, none.*

*I have been hunted down*
*to my last shape.*

*But in you, near the echoing*
*heart a silence, bear me.*
*I am*

*the icon of the incomplete*
*in you.  As I am, as I will*
*never be, live with me.*

(for music by Stephen Paulus)

# THE THING ITSELF

---

## AT THE JEWISH MUSEUM

*"Kaddish for the Little Children." An environment,*
*consisting of a room 28 x 17 x 8 ft.  By Harold Paris.*

Only what I bring to this room will exist here.
For the room is empty.
Empty as the inside
of a cold oven.
Narrow passageway in.
Narrow passageway out.
At the entrance, bronze scrolls.
Words:
the alphabet of mysterious
tablets.
May words guide me through this place.

Enter.
Did I expect to find
darkness?
Did I hope for
blindness?
Worse then absence of light this
gloom and glint of some
metal object.  Is it
a box?
A receptacle for —
what?
An artifact
of a door in the mind?
(Metal door that
clangs, clangs —     )
Walls bare,
Naked bricks.
Nothing to see.
Nothing.

In this room there were never clocks or calendars
or daily lists of little things to be done.
No one ever had any birthdays.
No one ever put on a hat.
Neither star nor spider came here.
Nor mouse nor cricket.
There is no trace of the memory
of a swirl of dust
of a fly
crawling on the wall.
A room without history of furniture
of broken plates or cups
of diaries
lost buttons
of shreds of cloth
of colors.
A room filled with absence
a room filled with loss
a room with no address
in a city in a country
unknown to mapmakers.

Once and only once
God
a trembling old man leaning on a cane
passed by but did not dare
look in.

Perhaps the bricks know something.
Perhaps the black metal object
is a box with names.
Perhaps nobody had a name.
It was all done with numbers.
It meant less that way.
Perhaps the box is filled with numbers.
Perhaps the walls and ceiling —
shadow walls and shadow ceiling
bulging with emptiness

*are receding rapidly to the edge*
*of the visible universe where objects*
*tend to disappear —*
where all the names have gone
the diminutives
the sweet
nicknames
beyond reach of our most cunning
telescopes
and nets to catch the whispers
of the stars.

## PENTIMENTO
*for an art student*

you were meticulous as a sculptor
smoothing right angles chip by tiny chip
finding the contour of a thigh
in the middle of a straight-edged block —
a slip of the chisel mattered
a piece once removed
could not be replaced

now you sit at the easel
and compose, adding
layer upon layer of paint —
mistakes no longer matter
a slip of the brush is soon buried

tomorrow i will show you
"Arnolfini Wedding" by Van Eyck
with the shadow of a leg showing through
the layer above meant to hide it

take up your chisel, risk a mistake
time sees through oil
marble hides nothing

## CHAIRS
### *after the Margaret Agnes Wharton show*

Take a chair. (This is going to take some time
To explain.) The artist takes a chair
And walks and talks about the seated chair
And feels the forest in the painted tree.

In the chair the artist sees another chair
And takes her saw and frees the other chair.
She separates the painted bars; the bark
Is kitchen colors and the artist peels

The chair like a summer vegetable and saves
The peel of paint and makes a hollow chair
Out of it. The hollow chair celebrates
The chair and shows its grain advantageously.

The artist takes another chair and sees
Two other chairs. The artist takes her saws
And slices the top and the bottom off
Of day-to-day existence. The chair folds

Along the lines of what the artist's saw
Felt in the chair. The artist's dentist's drill
Has opened teeth so that teeth may be filled
With floss that ties the artist to the chair.

The top and the front, the bottom and back
Conform to the bite of the artist's mind
But malocclude with the beautiful white
Chair of the chair that was never chewed up.

The artist takes a chair and takes a chair
Out of its side. She takes another chair
Out of its other side. She takes a chair
Out of its top, its bottom, its front, its back.

The artist shuffles a deck of chairs
And deals a chair.  The artist presses a straight
Between two jokers of plexiglass.
The artist does card tricks.  Take a chair, any chair.

The artist takes a chair from her front porch
And walks around the block with it.  She stops
Before her neighbors and asks for more chairs,
But everyone sits and makes his own chair sit

Still.  How those chairs want to fly to the artist's
Life-giving saw.  How those chairs want to feel
The pains of resurrection in their souls
Explode the souls of all who sit on them.

The artist returns to her kitchen chairs
And cores and pares another fruitwood chair
To square the three dimensions of her eye
And make a theatre of the gallery.

The artist sits still on a single chair
And soon she feels an audience of chairs
Around her.  And the chairs applaud their one
Creator and mirror their mother chair.

## THE DISCRIMINATIONS: VIRTUOUS AMUSEMENTS AND WICKED DEMONS

I.

Of Virtuous Amusements, i.e. good conditions, are numbered
the following:

a party of articulate lovers
a clean table
the season of tea, of bamboo shoots, of watermelon
a host who is not bold and severe
reading a great book slowly
sitting in the midst of landscape paintings
burning incense and cultivating fine manners
examining old masters
no need to close the window
a great monk in the snow (i.e., philosophical discussions)
to be surrounded by rare stones, wild flowers, hand-made vessels
recovering from illness
awakening from sleep
walking to the River
dry shoes
snowed in with friends
plenty of time to roll and unroll the pictures
strong men and sublime music
a clear sky with a beautiful moon —
        or as the translator of Bojang put it:
        "On top of Cold Mountain the lone round moon
        Lights the whole clear cloudless sky —
        Honor this priceless natural treasure
        Concealed in five shadows; sunk deep in the flesh."

II.
Of Wicked Demons, i.e. bad conditions, are numbered the following:

the unwilling horse
the season of yellow prunes
after drinking
inscriptions written in a confused way
a hurried visitor at one's side
too busy to watch the sun set
a room where water is dripping in
cares of the world
sneezing rats
to ask the price
pictures used for cushions
eaten by bookworms
caught by Mr. Inbetween
sad dreams in a fitful night's sleep
a handle that does not fit the socket
aching ears (i.e., idle talk)
broken shoe-laces
a hundred degrees in the trailer

III.
(Ch'ên Chi-ju goes on to distinguish the good and bad fates
that may befall a picture)

Here follow assorted bad fates which may befall a picture:
    to be scorched in a fire
    to fall into the hands of a jerk
    to be pawned
    to be buried in a tomb
    to be covered by glass
    to be cut up for roof patches

Here follow assorted good fates which may befall a picture:
    to be hung near a window at eye-level
    to belong to a literary courtesan
    to be placed in a sturdy frame
    to be named well
    to be admired by opened eyes
    to be painted by Fan K'uan, Raphael, Ray Morgan

IV.
Ch'ên Chi-ju's last words:

> From the grapples
> of Wicked Demons
> into the hands
> of Virtuous Amusements,
> Kuan-yin
> Deliver us.

By Ch'ên Chi-ju, Resident Fellow Confucian Institute of Correspondence, Ming (i.e. luminous) Dynasty, from his greatest work: the *Shu Hua Chin T'ang*. Assembled by Jim Bogan.

---

114

## HOLD MY HAND

Everything in the world has been photographed.
Everything.  The woods in the lake are taken
and the lake has refracted the woods.  Wind
shreds the water's reflection.  At night, Andromeda
glows in a time exposure.

We have photographed the vault in which the total
photography of the world is sequestered in darkness,
and all darknesses, too, we have documented;
and the light-sensitive silver inside earth; and all light
sailing from galaxies never beheld.

For we are artful and hungry to seize the light
that carves our camera skulls, endlessly confirming
distress and meditations of infants, lovers gazing,
soldiers waving from tanks, old people half-remembering
the violent deaths of presidents.

And the problem of what to do with all these pictures
is the same as where to secrete radioactive wastes,
how best to bury them, outlive them, deny them;
or the problem of how to elude certain memories,
of eyes with no mind behind them.

So cling to my silver halide hand and dance with me
in the light that blesses and gowns us
with singularity, and makes us poignant
to gods who don't mind being photographed,
who have the aplomb of models.

## CONVERSING WITH PARADISE
*For Robert Jordan*

To see the world the way a painter must,
Responsive to distances, alive to light,
To changes in the colors of the day,
His mind vibrating at every frequency
He finds before him, from wind waves in wheat
Through trees that turn their leaves before the storm,
To the string-bag pattern of the pebbles waves
Over the shallows of the shelving cove
In high sunlight; and to the greater wave —
lengths of boulder and building, to the vast
Majestic measures of the mountain's poise;

And from these modulations of the light
To take the elected moment, silence it
In oils and earths beneath the moving brush,
And varnish it and put it in a frame
To seal it off as privileged from time,
And hang it for a window on the wall,
A window giving on the ever-present past;

How splendid it would be to be someone
Able to do these mortal miracles
In silence and solitude, without a word.

## *I WALK ON THE RIVER AT DAWN*

Wind has grained the snow,
left it the unplaned texture of old boards.
Feet sensitive, I feel
the path I cannot see,
and shift aside the dust
blown deep in boot marks
on the water.  Even cliffs
and trees are different now and give up
secrets unrevealed in summer.  Far
from here, you cut with knives into a block
and ink it, phase on phase of changes
blacked to show a winter's texture,
to create by printing what the wind
proves here.  In pale light
that shifts from north to east
I walk the water thinking of your print,
unlike, and yet as like as this will be
when I remember:  how the cold
burned down the canyon, how I wept,
my face north into the blade of wind.

## POSTCARD FROM ZAMBOANGA,
### For George Ramos

*Pain has an element of Blank—*
*It cannot recollect*
*when it began—or if there were*
*A time when it was not—*
                              *Emily Dickinson*

*So far, so good—though pain increases.*
*I need the distraction of painting . . .*
                              *Postcard from GR*

1.
Off Mindanao    warm salt wind
wrinkles the green/blue sea
casting its net of light
over the drowned sand

Two outriggers under carnival sails
ride in across the shallows    straddle
the surface like waterstriders
on Lake Sultan Alonto

Pain needs distraction    something
bright to look at    like these
sails    dazzling quilts    appliquéd
held up to the wind    Pain
needs distraction    it needs to
get its mind off you    or it might
recollect that time when
it was not

2.

Manuel Arguilla wrote his Luzon stories
in English     but in 1944
hiding on Mount Cauitan     he cut his hands
on the dark rocks     Japanese soldiers
caught him     that night needing distraction
from Pain
Manuel Arguilla found a clean page in his
mind and began a story     perhaps it went
like this:     *Two outriggers under carnival sails*
*ride in across the shallows, straddle the*
*surface like waterstriders on Lake Sultan Alonto*
but Pain left Manuel
Arguilla at the instant     his head left
his body     taking with it     the merest
beginning of     a     story

3.

On the beach near Zamboanga
your clean sheet of one hundred forty pound coldpress
watercolor paper
reflects the sun     you move
under the palm tree's collection of
shadows     dip the new brush into
cobalt violet     loosen
the wet paths of vermillion     chrome yellow
lampblack     guiding them into place
around the empty white triangles in the design

Their carnival sails
stiffening under your brush     these outriggers
blow toward the edge
of the paper     Pain     the element of Blank
turns     just in time to wave

## ONLY ONE
### — *After a painting by Georgia O'Keeffe*

A dried blowfish crumbling now, a pocket
watch hung in a glass bell, two gold teeth,
legends that pile up on the earth
like snow, blue sounds in a cold field,
telephone wires singing in fours . . . these,
and the axle I meant to replace drying in the sun
like flat horns of a brained calf, these things
happen twice — even in Amarillo, Texas where
the only thing going is the wind, a few
strings, a little string music. Here
Georgia O'Keeffe was just a little girl by
the fence and the fence spoke back. "Hon,"
it began in big orange vowels, "make
me what I really am — far off, clandestine, away beyond."
"No," said the little girl, "no, no, no, no, no."

# THE PHOTOGRAPHER WHOSE SHUTTER DIED

He cannot help it that his only eye
decided to close for good,
cannot help it that the flashpowder world
became too bright.
His camera is this dark womb
he carries with him everywhere.

The image of everything he's focused on
stays locked inside—
each memory exact, each scene
exposed perfectly,
down to the sharp edge of weeds.

He curses himself for the thousand times
he looked but never saw, the times
when everything moved and he still
refused to focus, the times
he welcomed swirling dust.

Sometimes he thinks he hears the faces
caught inside the camera calling out his name—
a sound like voices traveling through granite.
But to open the cover
would smear their faces with black paint.
He stares into the lens,
sees only the reflection of his own filmy eye
that he cannot stop from staring
all the way to the back of his brain.

## CARVED BY OBADIAH VERITY

Once when I was looking at some decoys
carved a hundred years ago,
curlews and plovers, ruddy turnstones,
I thought of how they began,
as stutters in wood, gouges and flutes,
skewers and judgments of beauty.

They were simple things,
in their heartwoods the grains ran on,
the primitive music of fibers.
And as I stood there I began to imagine
Verity working, the acts of his hands,
the pauses, in which he kept

mounting something finer than skin
on those things. And what came over
the years was more than a touchable
silence. There was something
in those shore birds I was supposed
to pass on, from Verity,

like the deep intelligence of love,
and I left that place full of
breed, and brood, and cross-hatching.

## GHAZAL: JAPANESE PAINTBRUSH

This morning your hairs hurt with disuse, stiff,
Abused by some painter's cobalt jabs.

It is not solely the Red Sea which parts.
Another's liquid forms still waves, contained.

Ball and chain force open a stone-dry orifice —
For carpenters, tearing-down is creative, like fathering.

At dusk, fishing is best.
With feathers clinging, flies drag like brushstrokes on gray wash.

Bamboo stands hollow as bristled snakegrass in woody swamps.
Matisse breathes above his reed brush, while the paint clots and
      dries unused.

## HANGING SCROLL

I have come back to Princeton three days in a row
to look at the brown sparrow in the apple branch.
That way I can get back in touch with the Chinese
after thirty years of silence and paranoid reproach.
It was painted seven hundred years ago by a Southerner
who was struggling to combine imitation and expression,
but nowhere is there a sense that calligraphy
has won the day, or anything lifeless or abstract.
I carry it around with me on a post card,
the bird in the center, the giant green leaves
surrounding the bird, the apples almost invisible,
their color and position chosen for obscurity—
somehow the sizes all out of whack, the leaves
too large, the bird too small, too rigid,
too enshrined for such a natural setting,
although this only comes slowly to mind
after many hours of concentration.

On my tree there are six starlings sitting and watching
with their heads in the air and their short tails under the twigs,
They are just faint shapes against a background of fog,
moving in and out of my small windows
as endless versions of the state of darkness.
The tree they are in is practically dead,
making it difficult for me to make plans
for my own seven hundred years
as far as critical position, or permanence.
—If the hanging scroll signifies a state
of balance, a state almost of tension
between a man and nature or a man and his dream,
then my starlings signify the tremendous
delicacy of life and the tenuousness of attachment.
This may sound too literary—too German—
but, for me, everything hangs in the balance
in the movement of those birds,

just as, in my painter,
his life may have been hanging from the invisible apple
or the stiff tail feathers or the minuscule feet.
I don't mean to say that my survival
depends upon the artistic rendering;
I mean that my one chance for happiness
depends on wind and strange loyalty and a little bark,
which I think about and watch and agonize over
day and night,
like a worried spirit
waiting for love.

## A MESSAGE TO THE PHOTOGRAPHER WHOSE PRINTS I PURCHASED
*for Bruce Johnson*

*"The camera makes everyone a tourist in other people's reality, and eventually in one's own."*
On Photography *by Susan Sontag*

This is to let you know
I have hung your prints
on my wall . . . that is,
they are here, side by side,
the strange white expanse
that dominates each
to the inside, creating
a ghost lake between them.

At times I forget
they are on the wall.  What I mean
is, I forget the wall is there.
Large in the beginning
they seem to be growing, taking over
not only the wall but the room.

I find myself in this room
visiting them more and more often,
held as fast by their white spaces
as they are to my white wall.
Yes, suspended, I find
I can live there, pack in for days.
I'm beginning to question
which was the purchaser, which
the purchased . . . and what the real cost.

I had decided
not to buy them, you know,
realizing their dark silhouettes
might prove too hard
for these soft-hued rooms
but I returned,
drawn . . . oh, by the shorelines
I love, driftwood, and that water
lapping the sand
like a painter's wave . . . but mostly
by those spaces
created by diminishment
of the subtler shades

and we came away together,
I and those black bone trees,
dark logs floating in whiteness
that could be sky
as well as water
 . . . this whiteness
that splits open my walls
and extends forever in the distance,
no lines visible to inform me
where water and sky divide.

"Codalith, Type 3"
you called the process . . . the camera,
the brute instrument
in the photographer's hands
innocently revealing what is to be seen

but the process we choose
makes the difference, innocently
(perhaps) revealing what is —
this, and nothing less —
this, and nothing more —

the sharp contrasts,
our bone selves
etched in ebony against
unknowable space,
searching forever the mist, the mystery of whiteness, the blind eye of color
that holds all colors hidden
within itself.
        They are here —
your specially processed photographs,
but (this is the real message) I
do not have
them.
        If you need to respond
to this message, address me in care of
the vast spaces in your photographs.
I may be found drifting there
and I may not —
(my canoe — light, my hair
turning white).

## DRAWINGS BY CHILDREN

I

The sun may be visible or not
(it may be behind you,
the viewer of these pictures)
but the sky is always blue
if it is day. If not,
the stars come almost within your grasp;
crooked, they reach out to you,
on the verge of falling.
It is never sunrise or sunset;
there is no bloody eye
spying on you across the horizon.
It is clearly day or night,
it is bright or totally dark,
it is here and never there.

2

In the beginning, you only needed
your head, a moon swimming in space,
and four bare branches;
and when your body was added,
it was light and thin at first,
not yet the dark chapel
from which, later, you tried to escape.
You lived in a non-Newtonian world,
your arms grew up from your shoulders,
your feet did not touch the ground,
your hair was streaming,
you were still flying.

## AFTERBIRTH
### *(Sculpture#4—Bronze)*

Each creation
drawn from the deep hot kiln
of the heart
is beautiful    beautiful

and this white substance
that we wipe
from the nostrils
and eyes    whether fluid
or dust
is sacred
We should bury it
with prayer
lifting the new thing
carefully up

being not too quick
to cut it free
from cords
that nurtured its beginnings

not too anxious
for the cooling to begin
for the soft parts to harden
for the fissures and flashings
that so distinctly mark
each particular creation's
imperfection
to be masked

This daughter's head
I have born to air once
and twice more
through clay and wax
offers now this fourth blessing
in bronze    Oh
the divine imperfections
such flesh    such bones    allow
the heart and hands to repeat

## *INSTEAD OF FEATURES*

For Sudek, this is sex,
a face obscured. Instead
of features, a head of curls.

The mouth's line, though, is there;
tight, withdrawn, it hides
the slick probe of the tongue.

The breasts journey whitely—
pure as two newfallen eggs—
toward the dismissive black

Sudek chooses for flesh
to rest against.
The woman sits. The man looks

and puts a black border
square beneath her buttocks. This,
too, is sex: unfair, hidden

safe behind a lens.
Nakedness is cold
her clasped hands seem to say.

He has made her shoulders fall
under shadow. A bare light
rises from them as from

birches at night:
her shoulders shine, but
darkly. He has played a joke

on light. Darkness and light:
the model has no voice.
Her whole body speaks, bent

into dozens of vocal
curves.  Her elbow blurs
like thick fog above her thigh.

Sudek trusts the blur of things.
The body is a dusk.
When he walks there

among the darkening limbs,
stars appear, and he sees how
nipples are everything

he will never understand.
He blurs them gently, until
they merge with the blackness

which surrounds her body.  He
makes a game of dusk.
The face hides, the nipples

reveal confusion.  This is
life that Sudek swings before us
like a game, like a body

on a chain, like a nameless
ambivalence.  There is
no other way, his camera

says again and again.  Live
for the lens, its gift
of the border, where

even the longest dusk
loses its curve, and even
the body must finally end.

## THE PAINTER DREAMING IN THE SCHOLAR'S HOUSE
*in memory of the painters Paul Klee*
*and Paul Terence Feeley*

I

The painter's eye follows relation out.
His work is not to paint the visible,
He says, it is to render visible.

Being a man, and not a god, he stands
Already in a world of sense, from which
He borrows, to begin with, mental things
Chiefly, the abstract elements of language:
The point, the line, the plane, the colors and
The geometric shapes.  Of these he spins
Relation out, he weaves its fabric up
So that it speaks darkly, as music does
Singing the secret history of the mind.
And when in this visible world appears,
As it does do, mountain, flower, cloud and tree,
All haunted here and there with the human face,
It happens as by accident, although
The accident is of design.  It is because
Language first rises from the speechless world
That the painterly intelligence
Can say correctly that he makes his world,
Not imitates the one before his eyes.
Hence the delightsome gardens, the dark shores,
The terrifying forests where nightfall
Enfolds a lost and tired traveler.

And hence the careless crowd deludes itself
By likening his hieroglyphic signs
And secret alphabets to the drawing of a child.
That likeness is significant the other side
Of what they see, for his simplicities
Are not the first ones, but the furthest ones,
Final refinement of thought made visible.
He is the painter of the human mind
Finding and faithfully reflecting the mindfulness
That is in things, and not the things themselves.

For such a man, art is an act of faith:
Prayer the study of it, as Blake says,
And praise the practice; nor does he divide
Making from teaching, or from theory.
The three are one, and in his hours of art
There shines a happiness through darkest themes,
As though spirit and sense were not at odds.

II

The painter as an allegory of the mind
At genesis.  He takes a burlap bag,
Tears it open and tacks it on a stretcher.
He paints it black because, as he has said,
Everything looks different on black.

Suppose the burlap bag to be the universe,
And black because its volume is the void
Before the stars were.  At the painter's hand
Volume becomes one-sidedly a surface,
And all its depths are on the face of it.

Against this flat abyss, this groundless ground
Of zero thickness stretched against the cold
Dark silence of the Absolutely Not,
Material worlds arise, the colored earths
And oil of plants that imitate the light.

They imitate the light that is in thought,
For the mind relates to thinking as the eye
Relates to light.  Only because the world
Already is a language can the painter speak
According to his grammar of the ground.

It is archaic speech, that has not yet
Divided out its cadences in words;
It is a language for the oldest spells
About how some thoughts rose in the mind
While others, stranger still, sleep in the world.

So grows the garden green, the sun vermillion.
He sees the rose flame up and fade and fall
And be the same rose still, the radiant in red.
He paints his language, and his language is
The theory of what the painter thinks.

III

The painter's eye attends to death and birth
Together, seeing a single energy
Momently manifest in every form,
As in the tree the growing of the tree
Exploding from the seed not more nor less
Than from the void condensing down and in,
Summoning sun and rain.  He views the tree,
The great tree standing in the garden, say,
As thrusting downward its vast spread and weight,
Growing its green height from dark watered earth,
And as suspended weightless in the sky,
Haled forth and held up by the hair of its head.
He follows through the flowing of the forms
From the divisions of the trunk out to
The veining of the leaf, and the leaf's fall.
His pencil meditates the many in the one
After the method of the confluence of rivers,
The running of ravines on mountainsides,

And in the deltas of the nerves; he sees
How things must be continuous with themselves
As with whole worlds that they themselves are not,
In order that they may be so transformed.
He stands where the eternity of thought
Opens upon perspective time and space;
He watches mind become incarnate; then
   He paints the tree.

IV

These thoughts have chiefly been about the painter Klee,
About how he in our hard time might stand to us
Especially whose lives concern themselves with learning
As patron of the practical intelligence of art,
And thence as model, modest and humorous in sufferings,
For all research that follows spirit where it goes.

That there should be much goodness in the world,
Much kindness and intelligence, candor and charm,
And that it all goes down in the dust after a while,
This is a subject for the steadiest meditations
Of the heart and mind, as for the tears
That clarify the eye toward charity.

So may it be to all of us, that at some times
In this bad time when faith in study seems to fail,
And when impatience in the street and still despair at home
Divide the mind to rule it, there shall be some comfort come
From the remembrance of so deep and clear a life as his

Whom I have thought of, for the wholeness of his mind,
As the painter dreaming in the scholar's house,
His dream an emblem to us in this life of thought,
The same dream that then flared before intelligence
When light went forth looking for the eye.

# ADDITIONAL POEMS ABOUT THE VISUAL ARTS
A Selected Annotated Bibliography
*by Phyllis Janik*

This is a collection of poems about works of art — visions reflecting landscapes, the artist's immediate material or imagined surroundings. The first such instance of a poet contemplating an artist's work occurs in the *Iliad*. Homer describes each panel of Achilles' shield while Hephaestus forges its myriad scenes. The poems in this book belong to that tradition of iconic poetry (the Greek *icon* as idea or image), reflecting as they do the writers' own ideas, images and landscapes.

Many references will be made to Jean H. Hagstrum's landmark study, *The Sister Arts: The Tradition of Literary Pictorialism and English Poetry from Dryden to Gray* (University of Chicago Press, 1958), since her work is a detailed historical analysis of the relationship between poetry and painting. As Hagstrum comments, the best iconic poetry realizes the idea of *ecphrasis*, the spontaneous dialogue between the viewer and what is seen. Through the poet, an otherwise mute landscape speaks. The eloquence of the painting reflects the ability of the poet who is eliciting the response. The passion of such encounters has varied through history, and has frequently been tempered by the critical prejudices of an age. In fleshing out the literary movements of various centuries, Hagstrum reveals the particular relation — always a close one — between poetry and painting, colored by a wide palette of tightly structured philosophies.

Hagstrum traces the evolution of literary-pictorial theory from Classical Antiquity to English Neoclassicism. In reviewing classical criticism, she cites Plato's reverence for sight as the most godlike of the senses, as well as crediting his Garden of Essences for giving us the image of visual abstractions in feminine forms, personifying art and literature. Aristotle's and Horace's influences are considered next, especially Horace's famous phrase, *ut pictura poesis*, "As sometimes in painting, so occasionally in poetry." Hagstrum emphasizes: "There is no warrant whatever in Horace's text for the later interpretation: 'Let a poem be like a painting'."

HOMER, *The Iliad*, xviii, the shield of Achilles.

*Greek Anthology*, trans. W.R. Paton, ("Loeb Classical Library"), London, 1927 (comments on various statues, including the Colossus of Rhodes, and Myron's famous bronze of a heifer).

VIRGIL, Aeneid, i, 446 ff (the Temple of Juno); vi (the temple of Apollo); viii (the personification of the Tiber and the shield of Achilles, among others).

HORACE, *Ars Poetica*, ll.361 ff.

OVID (Publius Ovidius Naso), *Metamorphoses*, tr. John Dryden (Pygmalion).

The Christian era of literary pictorialism contained two major strains, Hagstrum contends: one exemplified by Chaucer who adopted the conventions of Virgil and Ovid, while at the same time producing verbal renditions of contemporary arts and crafts, as in his description of the Temple of Venus in the *House of Fame*; the other, uniquely Christian, unites prayer and art by virtue of its desire "to speak to the object, to implore it, and to induce it to respond" (Hagstrum, p. 49). Art for the Christian was, as seen in the Christian epigrams in *The Greek Anthology*, an intermediary between the human and the divine. Dante "embodies both strains of medieval pictorialism" for Hagstrum. She cites Book X of the *Purgatorio* as evidence of the classical; and religious iconic poems in passages of the *Paradiso*.

The Renaissance, with its competitions between poetry and painting, provides an interesting precedent for our contemporary society's movement from verbal to visual high-tech. In Renaissance Italy and England, the knowledge of perspective and anatomy gave painting an ability to produce a truly faithful recreation of the natural world. The poetry of Shakespeare and Spenser embodied the most sophisticated pictorialism, and the tradition of the Elizabethan and Jacobean masque, as exemplified by Ben Jonson, was a merging of the visual and the verbal transmitted to later centuries.

The seventeenth, the Baroque century, in England and Italy, saw the epigram, inscribed on statues, tombs and urns, reunited with art object and altered to encompass the emblem. The poems of George Herbert create actual visual designs, as illustrated by the "Collar," "Pulley," "Windows," "Church-floor," and "Church Monuments," to name some. Baroque paintings were "encouraged to be literary; poetry, to be painterly." And both "to look beyond the canvas" to give "a total human response, religious, ethical, emotional" (Hagstrum, p. 101). The Italian poet Giambattista Marino's *La galeria del Cavalier Marino: Distinta in pittura & sculture* is a poetic gallery of specific paintings and sculptures. Marino's book is a milestone because it considered the poem as "stimulated by the art object but independent of it" (Hagstrum, p. 103). Andrew Marvell's "The Gallery," although following Marino's concept and title, concentrated into seven stanzas, is a "gallery in the soul" combining "the psychological and the pictorial (Hagstrum, p. 114, 116).

Neoclassic writers preferred literary/pictorial values which had been adopted by the Renaissance and originally practiced in Greece. Curiosity and enthusiasm created audiences familiar with poetry, painting, the sciences, and philosophy; therefore, one could make allusions freely. Hagstrum (p. 144) suggests three specific poetic inclinations: use of form and attitude reminiscent of classical sculpture; "imitating the history and mythology of pictorial art; and creating allegorical personifications recalling the icons and images of the graphic arts." Specific references include:

ALEXANDER POPE: Hagstrum suggests that poetic passages refer to specific paintings known to the poet/ painter. "Eloise to Aberard" (11. 163-70) to Albrecht Dürer's *Melancholy I*; "The Rape of the Lock" (Canto I, 11 121-42) to Titian's *Young Woman at Her Toilette*, and *Venus with a Mirror*, and to Rubens' *Toilette of Venus*.

JAMES THOMSON, *Seasons*. Hagstrum details the reference in "Spring" (revised, final version) to Guido Reni's fresco, *Aurora* (p. 260).

THOMAS GRAY, "Elegy Written in a Country Churchyard" — Hagstrum suggests the last section of the poem, with its contemplation of an engraved tomb, is "strongly reminiscent of Nicolas Poussin's *The Shepherds of Arcady*". (p. 296)

Poets referred to as 'The Romantics' incorporated literal and pictorial landscape into their work, often including art objects and ruins. Two which come to mind are Percy Bysshe Shelley's "Ozymandias" and John Keats' "Ode On A Grecian Urn"; William Wordsworth's "Elegiac Stanzas Suggested by a Picture of Peele Castle, In a Storm" refers to Sir George Beaumont's *Peele Castle, In A Storm*; John Keats' "Epistle To John Hamilton Reynolds" and "Ode To A Nightingale," refer to Claude Lorrain's *Landscape with Psyche and Palace of Love*.

The late nineteenth century saw many poets, including the Pre-Raphaelite Brotherhood, publishing, simultaneously, posters and paintings referring to one of their poems and books, and vice-versa. Examples include Dante Gabriel Rossetti's *The House of Life* and "The Blessed Damozel" and Oscar Wilde's and Aubrey Beardsley's versions of *Salome*. Rossetti's *Sonnets on Pictures* includes "Our Lady of the Rocks" (da Vinci's *Madonna of the Rocks*); "A Venetian Pastoral" (a Giorgione painting); "Spring" (Botticelli's *Primavera*); and "The Holy Family" (Michelangelo's *Holy Family* or *Tondo of the Tribune*). Algernon Swinburne parodied Rossetti in a "Sonnet for a Picture."

In the work of twentieth century writers, one sees evidence of Wallace Stevens' observation: "All our ideas come from the natural world: trees = umbrellas," as well as of his startling "realism is a corruption of reality." A strong sense of the visceral as well as the dispensing with any pre-fabricated restrictions about philosophy, subject or scheme, establishes a *laisser faire* attitude — one neither fragmented nor specious, but offering instead diversity, plurality, the whole possible shebang. There is a large shift in emphasis from the landscape or the visual work itself to the perspective of the viewer, or poet. We have become aware that the shield of Achilles changes as we move from Homer's to Auden's contemplation of it. Similarly, Breughel's *Landscape with the Fall of Icarus* is a different painting when it speaks to us through Auden's rather than Williams' poem. And each remark, comment, poem increases the cosmic studio of selves. Modern and contemporary examples compel us to build an explosion of room additions for our literary-pictorial gallery:

W.H. AUDEN, "Musée des Beaux Arts" (Breughel's *The Fall of Icarus*; the horse image refers to Breughel's *The Massacre of the Innocents*); "The Shield of Achilles."

MARVIN BELL, "Homage to Alfred Stieglitz."

ELIZABETH BISHOP, "The Night Watch" (Rembrandt's painting of the same title).

LOUISE BOGAN, "Medusa."

HART CRANE, "Brooklyn Bridge: Proem."

e.e. cummings, "ponder, darling, these busted statues."

NORMAN DUBIE, "February: The Boy Breughel".

LAWRENCE DURRELL, "A Watercolor of Venice."

LAWRENCE FERLINGHETTI, "In Goya's Greatest Scenes We Seem to See" (Goya's *Disasters of War*).

THOMAS HARDY, "A Portrait" (Velasquez's *L'infante Marguerite*).

PHYLLIS JANIK, "Yvette Guilbert's Black Gloves" (Toulouse-Lautrec's painting of the same title); "The Coughing Architect of Taj Mahal."

DONALD JUSTICE, "On a Painting by Patient B of the Independence State Hospital for the Insane."

X.J. KENNEDY, "Nude Descending a Staircase" (Duchamp's painting of the same title).

JOHN LOGAN, "A Suite of Six Pieces for Siskind"; "Eight Poems on Portraits of the Foot" (for the photographer Aaron Siskind).

EDNA ST. VINCENT MILLAY, "The Cameo."

PAUL MONETTE, "Degas."

PABLO NERUDA, "The Heights of Macchu Picchu," VI-XII, esp. IX.

JOHN PECK, "Colophon for Lan-t'ing Hsiu-Hsi."

DOROTHY PETERSON, "Sestina from a Pawnee Tomb."

EZRA POUND, "Portrait d'une Femme."

JOHN CROWE RANSOM, "Painting: A Head."

MURIEL RUKEYSER, "Ajanta."

SIEGFRIED SASOON, "In the National Gallery."

ANNE SEXTON, "The Starry Night."

HUGH SEIDMAN, "The Making of Color."

KARL SHAPIRO, "The Dome of Sunday."

WALLACE STEVENS, "The Man with the Blue Guitar"; "Angels Surrounded by Paysans" (Tal-Coat, a still life); "St. Armorer's Church from the Outside"; "Anecdote of the Jar": "Study of Two Pears"; and numerous others.

MAY SWENSON, "O'Keeffe Retrospective."

HILARY TINDLE, "The Horse in Archaeology" (cave painting).

WILLIAM CARLOS WILLIAMS, "Pictures from Breughel," 1-9.

WILLIAM BUTLER YEATS, "Lapis Lazuli"; "On a Picture of a Black Centaur by Edmund Dulac."

## General References

*Geographies of the Mind*, ed. Lowenthal and Bowden, Oxford University Press, 1976.

E.H. GOMBRICH. *Ideals & Idols: Essays on Values in History & In Art*. Phaidon Press, 1979.

_____ *The Image & The Eye: Further Studies in the Psychology of Pictorial Representation*. Cornell University Press, 1982.

JEAN H. HAGSTRUM, *The Sister Arts. The Tradition of Literary Pictorialism and English Poetry from Dryden to Gray*. The University of Chicago Press, 1958.

ERWIN PANOFSKY. *Studies in Iconology: Humanistic Themes in the Art of the Renaissance*. Harper & Row (Icon Editions), 1972.

_____ *Idea: A Concept in Art History*. Harper & Row (Icon Editions), 1974.

_____ *Meaning in the Visual Arts*. University of Chicago Press, 1982.

WALLACE STEVENS, *The Necessary Angel*. Random House, 1965.

*Poems about Landscapes, Using the Techniques of Painting*

CID CORMAN, "Call It A Louse."

J.V. CUNNINGHAM, "Montana Pastoral."

PAUL GOODMAN, "The *Weepers' Tower* in Amsterdam."

GEORGE HITCHCOCK, "Three Portraits"; "Figures in a Ruined Ballroom."

DONALD JUSTICE, "The Snowfall"; "Landscape with Little Figures."

ARCHIBALD MACLEISH, "Landscape As a Nude."

THOMAS MERTON, "Elegy for the Monastery Barn."

THEODORE ROETHKE, "Root Cellar"; "Child on Top of a Greenhouse."

WALLACE STEVENS, "The Sense of the Sleight of Hand Man"; "Thirteen Ways of Looking at a Blackbird."

WILLIAM CARLOS WILLIAMS, "The Clouds"; "The Red Wheelbarrow"; "Tribute to the Painters"; "The World Contracted to a Recognizable Image."

# ALPHABETICAL INDEX OF AUTHORS

*Typeset in Bembo by duck type (Minneapolis, Minnesota).*
*Printed by Thomson-Shore, Inc. (Dexter, Michigan)*
*on Glatfelter acid-free paper.*

Emilie Buchwald's work has been anthologized in *The Minnesota Experience, 25 Minnesota Writers* and *Prize Stories: The O'Henry Awards*, among others. Her two award-winning fantasies are *Floramel and Esteban* and *Gildaen* (Harcourt Brace Jovanovich, Inc). She is the editor of *Milkweed Chronicle*.

Ruth Roston's book of poems, *I Live in the Watchmaker's Town* (New Rivers Press), was a winner of the 1981 Minnesota Voices project. She has taught in the Writers and Artists in the Schools program for the past six years. Her poems have been widely published and frequently anthologized. She was a 1981 participant in The Loft Mentor series.

Randall W. Scholes has illustrated numerous books of poetry, the most recent of which is *Moon* (1984), a letterpress edition by Bieler Press. Artist and graphic designer, he is at work on a series of wood engravings. Scholes is art editor of *Milkweed Chronicle*.

Phyllis Janik's latest book of poems is *No Dancing / No Acts of Dancing*, published by BkMk-University of Missouri (KC) Press in 1983. She has lectured frequently on the relationship between poetry and the visual arts.